GW01377220

GROWING PAINS

Trained as a nurse and midwife and winner of a Gold Medal for outstanding achievement, Claire Rayner's expertise and knowledge has been put to good use in her books. She has written over sixty, including books on sex education for children and adults; home nursing; family health, and baby and childcare, as well as fiction.

She has contributed important articles to most UK national newspapers and many leading magazines. She is now acknowledged as a leading 'Agony Auntie', having written a teenage problem page for a number of years, and *The Sun* problem page for seven years. Her page in *The Sunday Mirror* and the advice work she does for Capital Radio and BBC TV attract thousands of letters each year from all ages and both sexes.

GROWING PAINS

And How To Avoid Them

Claire Rayner

Illustrations by David English

Heinemann·Quixote

**To
Sylvia and her quartet
Who no longer need these pages**

Heinemann/Quixote Press
10 Upper Grosvenor Street
London W1X 9PA

LONDON   MELBOURNE   TORONTO
JOHANNESBURG   AUCKLAND

Copyright © Claire Rayner 1984

Flowcharts by Julia Alldridge Design

434 98042 0

Printed in Great Britain by
Redwood Burn Limited, Trowbridge, Wiltshire

CONTENTS

	Introduction	1
1.	You And Your Body	3
2.	You And Your Personality	43
3.	You And Your Parents	68
4.	You And Your Other Relatives	80
5.	You And Other People	92
6.	You And Your Friends	103
7.	You And Your Problems	116
8.	You And Your Love Life	139
9.	You And Your Plans For The Future	171
	Information Section	188

INTRODUCTION

Ask most adults what children need to be taught and you'll probably be given lists of school subjects. Reading and writing and arithmetic. French and Latin and history. Biology and physics and chemistry.

But useful though these subjects are (sometimes) they are far from being the most important matters for young people. What you really have to do while you move through the years that take you from helpless baby to independent adult is learn how to cope with the world that belongs to you. It's a very complex world, stuffed as it is with people all wanting the best for themselves all the time, and run by organisations and systems that are as tangled as a bowl of spaghetti, but it *is* your world. Or will be. And you need a lot of information and guidance on how to make the best of it.

But, because a large number of adults suffer from severe amnesia, and have forgotten what it was like to be young and trying to grow up well, not enough of this information is offered to young people. It's taken for granted that you'll find out for yourselves how to sort out your feelings and needs, how to identify and then solve your emotional problems, how to deal with other people. And of course, most young people do. All the capable adults you see around you were once in their early teens and trying to make sense out of their world. And they managed it.

But it takes time to find out by yourself (and some people never do; they are the uncapable adults you see around you) and it can be a very painful business. Over and over again adults say, "If I'd only known what I know now when I was younger —"

That is why this book has been written. To help you discover while you're still quite young some of the strategies of adult living so that when you become an adult you'll enjoy it more. The book is designed to help you learn how to understand yourself (and that's a task that some adults have never been able to complete) and then how to understand

2   Growing Pains

the other people in your life. How to cope with the many situations you'll land in and how to avoid falling into the more unpleasant kinds.

No book of course can provide all the answers to living. Every individual has to grow up in his or her own way; the only experience worth having is your own. But as with any travelling, it helps enormously to have a map prepared by someone who has made the journey before you. That is what this book is meant to be — a map to see you on your way.

Have a good trip.

CHAPTER ONE

YOU AND YOUR BODY

The most important person in your world is yourself. After all, it's through your eyes you see other people, through your ears you hear them, through your feelings you relate to them. So, it's obvious that you can't understand and care about other people until you understand and care about yourself.

There are some people who will say it's selfish and big-headed to be deeply interested in your own feelings and needs, but I don't think it is. All the really big-headed, boring, bumptious couldn't-care-less types I've met have turned out to be very unhappy people who were cringing inside and were putting on a big show of being self-confident. But the ones I've met who were relaxed and agreeable and fun to be with have always turned out to be people with real self-confidence and a healthy self-esteem — a genuine liking and respect for themselves.

So, getting to know yourself is important. How do you do it?

You're made up of several different strands. There is your body, there is your mind, there are your emotions and there is your personality. Each of these changes and develops as you leave childhood behind, but they don't change so totally that you become unrecognisable. It's extraordinary that caterpillars become butterflies, not at all extraordinary that babies become children and then adults. You can see the shadow of the person to come when you look in a baby's face, just as you can see the shadow of the baby that has long since gone when you look at an old man.

Which means that it's never too soon to start discovering about yourself, and never too late either. Whatever you discover, you add on to the store of self-knowledge you already have, and you can go on using it for the whole of your life.

4 *Growing Pains*

How to use this book

Depending on your age, and the sort of education you have had and are having, there will be some information in these pages which you already know. You may not want to read it all again, therefore. The next section, which deals mainly with the nuts and bolts of sex education — the way bodies change as people grow up — is an example. So by all means skip it and go on to something else.

And, of course, there will be some material aimed mainly at boys or mainly at girls. Some people may choose to miss out the sections that deal with the other sex; they'll be missing a lot if they do. It's as useful surely for girls to understand boys as it is for them to understand themselves — and vice versa.

Your body

Understanding how your body works is easy. This is because you can see the changes that happen. You can't see the changes in your personality and your mind as they grow; you can only feel them. But when you grow hair where you used to be smooth, become hard where you used to be soft, rounded and interesting where you used to be flat and plain, you can see and touch and smell the difference.

It is also easy to understand because although every individual is unique — there can't ever be two exactly matching people, even if they're identical twins — the patterns of growth through which people pass as they move from childhood to adulthood are much the same. Each person's growth will happen in its own unique way, at its own unique rate, to give its own unique finished product. But the rhythm of it will be the same. So, you can find out about your own changes by discovering about what happens to other people.

The physical changes

The rate at which each child grows depends on a number of different things. Inheritance comes into it. Small parents tend to produce small children. The child of a jockey who married a girl as small as he is will be a much smaller person that the child of a six-foot-two lumberjack who married a girl who matches him.

But environment matters as much as heredity. The way you're fed and cared for, and the way you're loved and cherished, has a great deal to do with how you grow. (Babies who are not adequately loved — being reared in nurseries — grow more slowly than babies cared for by their own loving mothers, even if they get the same sort of food.)

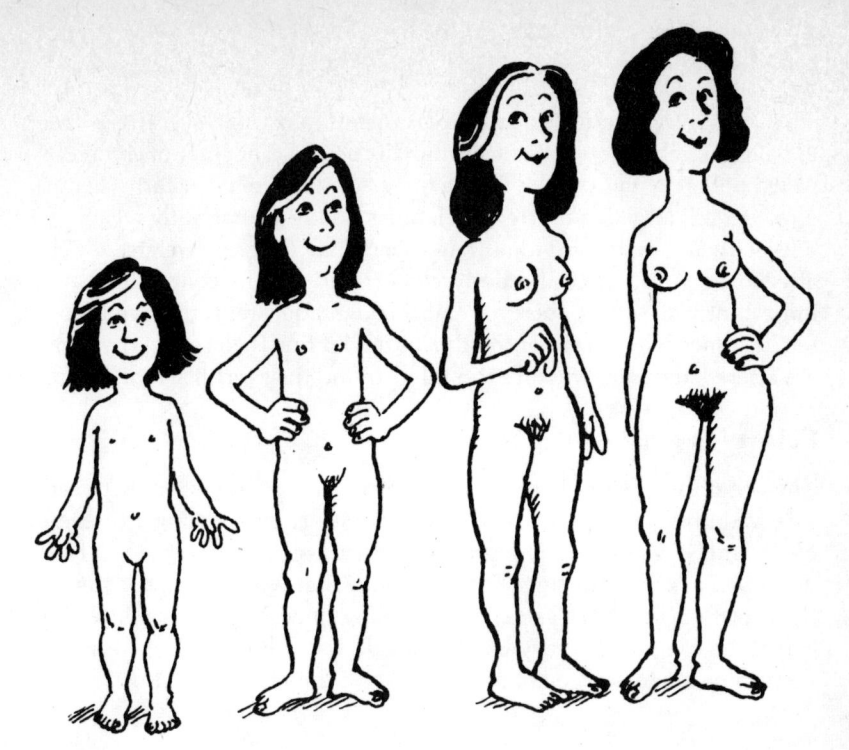

Girls Growing Up

AGE 5+
The small girl is hairless, smooth, straight. Head hair is fine, skin is usually clear. Sweat does not smell heavily even on unwashed child.

AGE APPROX. 10+
The hypothalamus starts puberty, sending out special stimulation to the pituitary which via its hormones affects other glands, especially adrenals and ovaries. By the action of their hormones fat is laid down over the hips, over the breasts, on upper arms and thighs. Pubertal girls may become quite plump; "puppy fat". The ovaries cause the breasts to grow — small hard areas appear under nipples which begin to enlarge. There may be some growth of the inner lips of the vulva which causes itching. Head hair becomes thicker, less fine than in babyhood. Vaginal discharge — thin, whitish — heralds the first period, the shedding of the inner lining of the uterus, which happens each month or *thereabouts*. (Cycles are usually uneven at start of puberty.) Two weeks after ovaries shed an egg.

AGE 12/13+
Breasts continue to enlarge, and may do so unevenly — one faster than the other. The second breast will "catch up" eventually though it is normal for one breast to be larger than the other all through life. Hair grows under arms, over genitals and may appear elsewhere — chest, arms, legs, belly. Sweat changes too — begins to smell "adult". This is all part of developing adult sexuality — body smell acts as an attraction in sexual relationships. Skin changes may result in acne, greasy hair.

AGE 17+
Adult sex development is complete within three years or so after first signs of puberty, but growth will continue for many years into late teens and twenties.

All this is important because size is one of the things that affects the age at which childhood ends and adult life begins. The stage of change is called puberty, and though all the factors that cause it to start when it does are still largely a mystery, scientists do know that body weight is one of them. Each individual has a personal "trigger" weight which affects the working of the body clock. And weight continues to be important well after puberty — all through adult reproductive life in fact. Women who get either too thin or too fat find their sexual rhythms are altered and men who are too fat also find their fertility is affected.

Puberty in girls

The age of onset of puberty varies enormously — anywhere between nine and fifteen is normal. And some people are even younger or even older, and still normal. The processes start inside the body up to two years before any clear signs can be seen. But at whatever age it starts, the process is much the same, though things may happen in a different order. As long as the various changes do begin however, there is no need to be anxious. If one happens, so will the rest.

Check List One

1. I am aged ten plus.
2. I am about the right weight — neither too fat nor too thin. (This has nothing to do with fashion by the way; fashionable models are *much too thin*. If you're in any doubt about whether your weight is about right for your height ask the school nurse, if she's available, or you can go to your doctor's surgery for him to check. But most people will be able to know by comparing themselves roughly with the rest of the class at school.)
3. My nipples are enlarging.
4. There are some firm pads of tissue under my nipples which are a little tender if I prod them.
5. I have a few hairs appearing over my pubic bone, and under my arms.
6. I'm sweating more and beginning to need to use a deodorant.
7. I have a little vaginal discharge — milky white stuff.
8. My skin gets greasier than it used to. I sometimes get spots.

9 My hair gets greasier than it used to, and needs washing more often.
10 Some of my skirts and trousers don't fit properly any more even though I haven't grown out of them — their shape seems all wrong.

If you answered yes to five or more of these, then puberty is on its way and your periods are likely to start in the next nine months to a year — maybe less.

STRATEGY
for periods

1 Go to your nearest self-service chemist's shop and look along the shelves where the sanitary towels and tampons are. Check the prices and the types. Look at the belts that can be used to hold sanitary towels in place, at the self-stick-to-ordinary-pants type, and also at the protective pants that can be used. Which do you think you'd be most comfortable in? Look at the tampons — see which ones have applicators and which have not (all the information is on the labels). Do you think you could use these?

2 Talk to a friend at the same stage of development, and see how she feels about these products. Also talk to your mother, older sister, aunts, if you feel comfortable doing so. But if these older people seem bothered, or tell you you're "too young" (even though it's obvious from your check list that you aren't!) choose a reliable teacher at school and talk to her. These discussions with experienced users of products for periods will help you decide which one you'd like to use yourself when the time comes.

3   Find a friend who is willing to choose a different method to yours (perhaps she wants to use a belt or pants and pad, and you'd prefer small tampons). Agree to equip yourselves with the gear of your choice, and later, to swop over — she tries one of your tampons, you try one of her pads — so that you get a chance to try both methods at the lowest cost. (For more information on the pros and cons of tampons, see the next section on "Questions Girls Ask".)

4   If possible ask your mother to finance you. If she can't, or doesn't feel it's necessary yet, then save up your own pocket money. Buy your first pack of pads and belt or tampons and put it away ready. The day you start your first period it's very helpful to have supplies at hand.

5   Study the diagram opposite about periods. Also have a look at some books on sex education. Get all the information you can about periods, and body changes. However, once you've read all you need to, *forget it*. To watch day in day out to see if your periods have started can get very tiresome — and boring. Remember it can be a year or so still before it actually happens.

Check List Two

1   I am aged eleven plus.
2   My nipples have enlarged considerably since this time last term.
3   I not only have firm pads of tissue under the nipples — I also have some increase of breast roundness.

You and Your Body 9

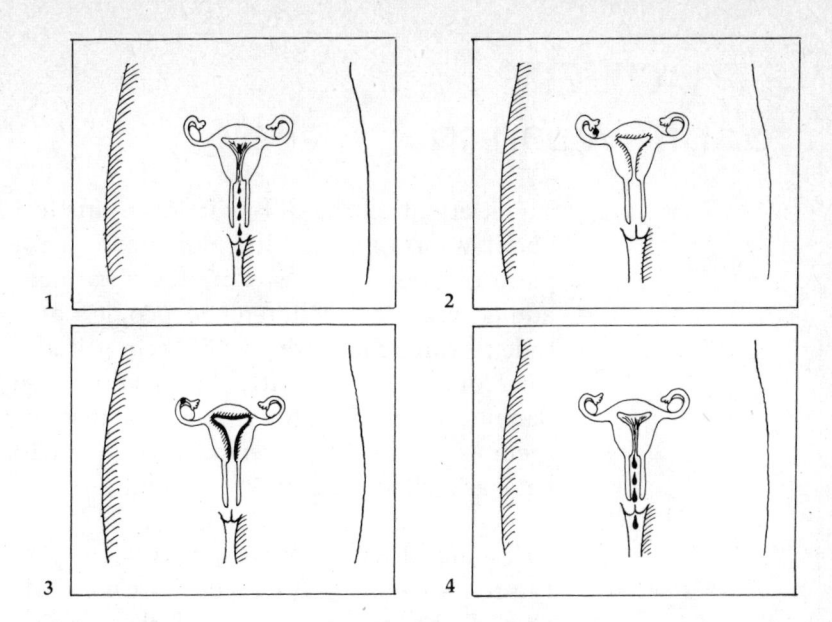

1	2
3	4

Periods
1. The cycle starts on the first day of a period, which lasts for about 5 days.
2. While the period lasts, and for about ten days afterwards, an egg slowly ripens in the ovary.
3. And at around the middle of the cycle, the egg is released to start its journey to the womb, via the tube. Meanwhile the womb lining thickens, becoming richer in blood, in case a fertilised egg arrives.
4. If the egg isn't fertilised, it arrives at the womb fourteen days after it was shed, and is thrown out, with the no-longer-needed lining and extra blood.
1. And we're back at Day 1 again.

---

4   When I run, and my breasts move on my chest wall, I ache a bit.
5   Lots of girls in my class are wearing a bra now.
6   I would like to wear a bra now.
7   Wearing a bra would make me feel silly and embarrassed.
8   I think bras are stupid — girls don't need them.

If you answered yes to questions 5 and 6 you're *emotionally* ready to wear a bra.

If you answered yes to question 7 then you're *not* emotionally ready to wear a bra.

If you answered yes to question 8, then you have *political* attitudes towards wearing a bra.

STRATEGY
for bra wearing

1. Think about all the different ways girls feel about wearing a bra. It's more than just a piece of underwear, isn't it? It's a garment adults wear, not children. So people's attitude towards them are part of their attitudes towards being an adult. This is why some parents are anti-bras for young girls; they see them as a sign that a person they prefer to have as a child is becoming an adult.

2. Ask yourself why girls wear bras.
   Is it to look more sexy? To be more comfortable? To be the same as all the other girls?
   Are these good reasons?
   To be more comfortable is, obviously. To be like everyone else is too, for those people who are only comfortable if they are part of the mainstream. To be "more sexy" isn't — because girls are sexy whether they wear bras or not.
   Breasts have no muscle fibres in them — only supporting tissue. Muscle fibres are elastic and go back to their original size after being stretched. Supporting fibres can eventually become over-stretched and won't go back to their original size. So, as time goes on breasts sag. It is to avoid this happening to their breasts that many women choose to wear bras. They help the supporting fibres.
   Do you think it is a good reason? (I can't possibly give you an answer to this question; only individuals can answer for themselves. Certainly there are no "right" or "wrong" answers; only your own opinion!)

3   Now be very practical and assess your own body type. If you are born to be large breasted, wearing a bra may be necessary for comfort, and never mind the politics. Heavy breasts can "drag" painfully if they are unsupported. If you are born to have small breasts, then you can choose whether to wear a bra at all, or as some women do, whether to wear a padded one which makes you look as though you've got bigger breasts than you really have.

4   If you are born to have small breasts (and it will be some years yet before you finish your breast development and can be sure) ask yourself whether you need to be ashamed of that fact, and whether wearing a padded bra will make you feel any better. Women are women, whether they have breasts as big as melons, or as small as poached eggs.
You are a whole person, not just a pair of breasts with a body tacked on behind.

5   In practice, most girls have bras given to them by — or withheld by — their mothers. In either case, go through this strategy list with your mother when the time comes, so that you feel comfortable with your decision.

Check List Three

1   I am aged eleven plus.
2   I am growing a lot of hair on my arms and legs as well as under my arms and over my pubis.
3   I have a little dark hair growing on my upper lip.
4   The other women in my family are like me, with hair on their arms and legs and upper lips.

If you answered yes to more than two of these, *and are worried by that fact* you may be thinking about dealing with the hair.

STRATEGY
for unwanted body hair

1. Why are you worried about the hair? Is it because other people have noticed it? Or is it just that *you* have noticed it? If no one else has ever noticed it, *it probably is not a problem*. Refuse to look for hairiness in future.

2. If it has been mentioned, then *do* take a look at others. Are you *sure* you really have a problem compared with the other brunettes (and don't look at blondes — this isn't usually an anxiety they have. They fret instead because their hair is thin or they have pallid eyelashes — there's always something). Was the person who suggested you were hairy just being unkind and critical? Are you in fact much like everyone else? (In my experience, this is the stage of the strategy at which most people stop — they agree they aren't really as unusually hairy as they thought.)

3. If you are still worried, discuss your anxiety about body hair with the older women in your family, who are the same. Does it worry them? Has it been a nuisance for them? Have they ever done anything about it? *Have they regretted doing anything about it?* (Lots of older women are bitterly sorry they ever started shaving or plucking unwanted hair, because it tends always to come back more thickly and coarsely).

4. If you're one of the few people who are really bothered by hair, and your older women

You and Your Body 13

> relations share your problem and agree it has helped them to get rid of it, then *seek expert guidance*. Do-it-yourself hair removal often leads to more problems than it solves — it can cause spottiness and scarring as well as heavy re-growth. Your family doctor may be able to advise medical treatment.

During puberty lots of girls have lots of anxieties — and no book could possibly answer everybody's individual questions. Some are sure to be left out. But here are some of the commoner ones I've been asked by girls aged twelve plus.

QUESTIONS
Girls Ask:

Question 1   "I think I've got a deformity. I have these two ugly wrinkled flaps of skin hanging down from my private parts. I know I'd never be able to marry and have children like this, because I'd be too ashamed to let anyone see them. Is there any operation I can have to get rid of them?"

Answer   This is a normal development. The vulva has a pair of thick fleshy outer lips, with in adult life hair growing on them, and inside them a pair of thin wrinkled inner lips. These are covered in membrane — like the inside of the nose or mouth — and are hairless. They have a Latin name: *labia majora* (big lips), and *labia minora* (little lips). At puberty the vulva starts to grow, including the little lips. Sometimes one lip grows bigger than the other. Sometimes they grow so long they stick out beyond the big lips. Some are wide and some are narrow. Just as people have different faces, so they have different vulvas — and each and every one makes its own unique pattern.

So you don't need surgery and you don't need to be ashamed or afraid of your own body. It's a lovely body, and it's all yours.

Question 2　"Whenever I see girls in tight T-shirts and see the way their nipples stick out I get so miserable, because mine only stick out like that sometimes, when I'm cold. All the rest of the time they're smooth and flat, and I feel so freakish."

Answer　You're normal too. Nipples are, like the clitoris and the penis, made of erectile tissue. It can be either smooth and floppy, or gathered up into a firm structure that stands up erect. Usually the nipples are smooth and flat, but when they're stimulated, up they rise. Stimulation can be cold, as you've discovered, or sexual excitement or the attentions of a hungry baby. This is why the nipples are erectile, of course — to make them easier for a baby to get hold of when he feeds. So, *you are normal.*

Question 3　"All the books say periods are supposed to happen every twenty-eight days. And they don't say they hurt. Mine come every five weeks and they often hurt a lot, so that I feel sick and want to go to bed. But everyone tells me not to fuss and that makes me feel worse."

Answer　Books can only talk about what is average. This book is talking about what is average, too. It's impossible to deal with everyone's individual differences, because we're all so special. In your case, thirty-five days is the normal cycle for you, *at present*. In the future your cycle may well change and become a twenty-day one. Or a thirty-one-day one. Or a totally irregular one so that you never know what's due and when. None of this matters, as long as it's your usual experience. It's sudden changes in menstrual rhythm that may, in older women rather than young girls (in whom irregularity and changes of pattern are common for the first few years of menstrual life), be medically significant. For example, a totally absent period in a sexually active woman may mean a pregnancy, and bleeding between periods in a middle-aged woman may mean the sort of potentially dangerous disease which needs checking; similarly unusually scanty or heavy periods may mean some underlying general illness that needs treatment. You can ask your doctor about problems like this. Otherwise, forget it. You're normal.

As to painful periods — well, they are for some people, not for others. And those who have no problems are often very unsympathetic to those who do. The answer is to try the various remedies that are available — starting with the simple ones.

1 Learn all you can about normal development. Girls who don't understand their own bodies, or who are fearful of adult sexuality may get tense and anxious. These anxious people sometimes tend to get painful physical reactions.

2 Eat a high-fibre diet to prevent any constipation. Some people have painful periods because the rectum, next-door neighbour to the uterus, is crowded with lumpy hard stools. Get rid of them and you'll get rid of the painful periods.

3 Try exercise. A sharp walk which gets all of your muscles working will help, sometimes, to relax belly muscles which encourage the uterus to go into painful cramps.

4 Take aspirin, according to the directions on the pack (usually one or two tablets no more often than four hourly, for no longer than 48 hours at a stretch). This drug not only limits pain; it also acts directly on body substances called prostaglandins which are involved in the painful cramps, nausea and diarrhoea some menstruating girls suffer.

5 If none of these work, see the doctor. Some girls need hormonal treatment — the Pill — to stop the pain. Others need other drugs, such as Ponstan (mefenamic acid); Meralen (flufenamic acid) or Naprosyn (naproxen).

16 *Growing Pains*

Question 4   "*I get this sticky white stuff coming out of my vagina. It makes my pants wet and it worries me. Is it VD?*"

Answer   VD — the modern label is "sexually transmitted disease" — may cause a vaginal discharge *but by no means all vaginal discharges are due to such disease*. Most of them are normal secretions leaking away. The vagina — the passageway from uterus to vulva — is meant to be moist. It makes its own slippery mucus, rather like the mucus made in the nose, to keep it soft and to act as a germ killer and as a cleanser; the secretion as it leaks away carries dust particles, germs and whatever else may have wandered in. In some people the discharge is heavy, and always means damp pants. Tiresome but harmless. Just change your pants more often or wear disposable pads to catch it.

In some people it's heavier at different times — just before periods is common, and also after being sexually aroused which increases vaginal mucus. As long as it is clear, smells normal — like your vulva usually smells — and dries to a powdery white on your pants, no need to fret.

However, it is far from uncommon for girls to pick up an infection called *thrush*. It's a yeast infection, and can happen to any woman, from tiny babies to old ladies, and from good-time girls to nuns. It is no respecter of persons. In this case, the discharge is creamy, thicker, heavier, smells nasty — a bit sour-milkish — and dries to yellowish stains on underwear and makes the vulva sore and achy. For this a doctor's treatment is needed. Do get it — and do use all the treatment he gives (probably cream or tablets to tuck into the vagina to dissolve there, or sometimes pills by mouth as well) because if you don't, you may make the yeast organism tougher and better able to resist treatment when it comes back. As it will, if you don't follow all instructions. Also, wear only *cotton* pants and/or open gussetted tights, and try not to wear jeans while you have thrush. The yeast thrives best in overheated moist conditions, which are increased in a vulva that is boxed in by non-porous underwear. Also, don't wash the vulva with soap, or use scented talc or sprays. Instead clean it with swabs soaked in olive oil B.P. (from any chemist) which soothes as well as cleans. Never panic about this condition. Thrush is so common it's unlikely there is a woman in the world who hasn't had it at least once — or will get it.

Question 5 "*I would like to use tampons when I have a period, so I can go swimming. My mum says girls who are virgins can't, but I know lots of girls who do, and they're virgins. Or aren't they? Mum also says they're unhealthy to use.*"

Answer Tampons are pledgets of compressed absorbent fibres which, tucked into the vagina during a period, catch the flow and save the bother of wearing surface pads. They're comfortable to use, unobstrusive and yes, you can easily swim during a period if you use them.

It is *not* true that virgins can't use them. The flap of membrane, called the hymen or maidenhead, which partially covers the opening of the vagina in young girls can usually be easily stretched to let a tampon in. Later, when a girl has intercourse and a penis enters the vagina — and an erect penis is much thicker than a tampon — the hymen is stretched so much it is said to be "broken". Once a girl has had intercourse and her hymen's been stretched by a penis, then she is said to have lost her virginity. Insertion of a tampon, however, is not a sexual experience and therefore does not change a girl's virginity. Lots of quite young girls — eleven or twelve — use them regularly.

As for health — there was a scare a while back about an illness called Toxic Shock Syndrome. In this, girls developed raging fevers and sometimes generalised "blood poisoning" because they had either used a tampon that dried the vagina out too much, so that dangerous germs could flourish there, or because they left a tampon in too long, and infection got in and again flourished undisturbed. But at the time of writing, research suggests that tampons are safe to use as long as they are changed frequently, and used in conjunction with surface pads, to allow the vagina time to "rest" between tampons. A night-time pad and day-time tampons changed at least three times during the day, would be best.

Question 6 *"Why can't you wash your hair when you have a period?"*

Answer But you can! This is one of the old wives' tales that upset a lot of people and for no purpose. There may have been some folk wisdom in its origins — like noticing that hair does become more unmanageable during a period, because of hormone changes, and blaming it on hairwashing which they could understand rather than hormones, which hadn't yet been discovered. Anyway, whatever the origin, we now know there is no harm in hair washing during a period, nor in bathing or swimming. If you want to swim, and don't want to use tampons, by the way, try a small surface pad, worn under close fitting plastic pants under a swimsuit. Unless the flow is heavy, there should be no leak, and no one will notice you're having a period.

Question 7 *"Every month, just before my periods start, I feel awful. I get headachy and I want to cry all the time and my clothes feel tight and I just have rows with people. As soon as my period starts I'm fine. My mum says this is normal and I just have to put up with it, but it's horrible."*

Answer Your mum is right that it's normal — well, very common, anyway — but not right that nothing can be done. If the premenstrual tension, which is its medical label, gets very severe then a number of things can be done.

The basic problem is that when the hormone balance changes during the menstrual cycle, there is a build up of fluid in the body. In some girls this causes no more than a temporary sense of being a little bloated. In others, however, it causes the sort of headache, misery, depression and discomfort you have. You can prove to yourself it's excess water that's the problem; as soon as your period starts, do you have to run to the loo more often to get rid of all the extra urine you're making? Almost certainly you do — it's the loss of the water that brings the relief.

The ideal answer is to prevent the fluid build-up. So, cutting down on salty foods, which encourage the body to retain fluid can help a lot. So can drinking a little less that you usually do. Some girls feel better if they take extra Vitamin B6 which can be bought at any chemist's shop as *Benadon,* or which a doctor can prescribe, and a few need hormone treatment.

It helps to keep a period diary so that you can actually see if you really get PMT — some girls who just get tense and anxious from time to time blame their periods when really it's nothing to do with them. If you do get PMT badly, tell the teachers at school, who may be able to help by arranging for important tests and so on to be done at a time when you're feeling more like your normal self.

There will, of course, be other questions you want answered which I haven't dealt with here; as I have already said, no one book can answer every single thing every person needs to know. Some of the answers you want may be later on in this section when I deal with questions that people of both sexes ask — for example, dealing with spots and weight anxieties. So keep on reading —

But first the problems boys have, as they reach puberty. Some girls may feel they can skip this part but I hope they won't.

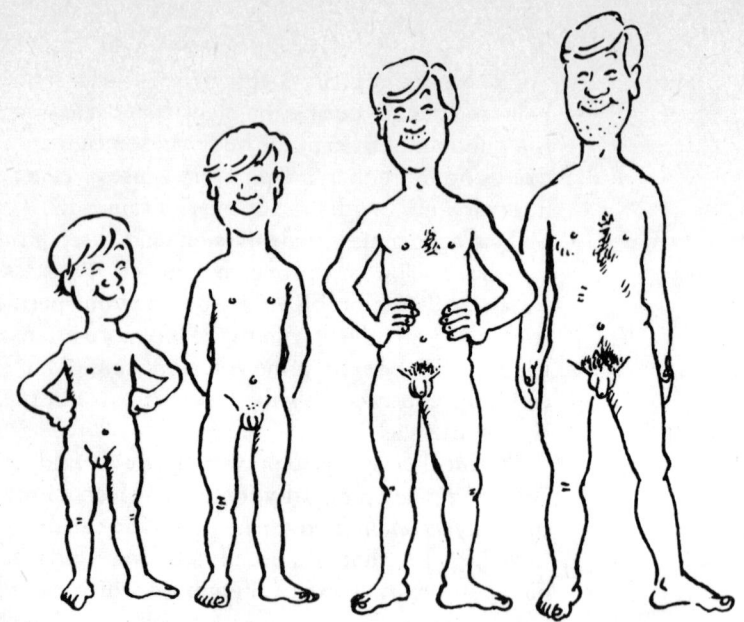

Boys Growing Up

AGE 5+
The small boy is smooth, hairless, high voiced. His skin is clear and his sweat is not offensive to smell.

AGE 11+
The first sign of puberty is usually growth of scrotum and testicles. Then the penis grows. Erections which have been happening all the boy's life, may become more frequent.

AGE 13/14+
There is a sharp growth spurt. Some boys grow three or four inches in as many months. Bones enlarge in width as well as length. The gawky look is increased by growth of facial bones. Hair grows at base of penis, may appear on belly, arms, legs. Nocturnal emissions — "wet dreams" — common.

AGE 17+
Strength is suddenly increased as muscles develop. Shoulders broaden. Hair growth may increase and it will appear on the face though some boys grow little body or facial hair. Voice deepens as larynx grows. Body and foot sweat smell stronger. Acne "spottiness" common as skin changes. Semen is increased in quantity and nocturnal emissions — "wet dreams" — increase.

Puberty in boys

As with girls the age of onset of puberty varies a great deal — with one difference. Boys lag behind girls; in them puberty starts later and takes longer than it does in girls. It can start between the ages of ten and sixteen and ends between fourteen and eighteen.

Check List One

1 I am aged twelve plus.
2 My scrotum and testicles (balls) and penis have grown.

3   I am having more erections than I used to.
4   I am having sexy dreams and when I wake up I find I am wet — I have produced some semen.
5   I am a lot taller than I used to be.
6   I am much stronger than I used to be.
7   My voice is unreliable — sometimes deep, sometimes not.
8   I am growing hair under my arms and over my penis.

If you answered yes to four out of these eight questions then your puberty is well on its way.

If you answered yes to fewer than four out of these eight DON'T PANIC. Some people do start as young as twelve — but lots not until they are fifteen or so.

Whenever it happens, the aspect of change that seems to worry most boys most is the rate at which penis and testicles grow.

STRATEGY
for growth

1   Try not to look at your sex organs critically too often. Take pride in what you have. It's yours and it's good.

2   When you compare yourself with other boys, when you see them in the showers at school for example, NEVER look down at yourself to compare. That way you get a foreshortened and meagre view. Always look in a mirror at your profile. You get a more accurate image that way.

3   Wear well-fitted underpants that hold your genitals comfortably without crowding them. You'll like the way you look in those more

than the way you look in baggy boxer style shorts. Later in life however, it might be better to change from firm underpants to loose ones; there is some evidence to show that testicles work better when they are cool, and men who want to become fathers and who have a reduced number of sperms often become more fertile if they wear the cooler, looser style.

4 Be assured that the size of the penis and testicles has no effect at all on virility. In most men the erect penis is much the same size — a penis which is on the small side enlarges more than one that is on the large side, so that both are about the same when fully ready for sex.

5 Don't fall for any con tricks that promise to enlarge the penis. There are ads in sexy magazines for all sorts of exercises and other tricks that are said to increase growth.
These are all lies.
There is no evidence that any such system works. Anyway, really undersized organs are *very very rare*. If you think you're one of the rare ones check with your GP. It's odds on he'll tell you you aren't.

Check List Two

1 I am fourteen plus.
2 I think a lot about sex.
3 I often have erections — just looking at a TV film, or seeing a good looking person in the street, or even just riding in a bumpy bus.
4 I have wet dreams.
5 I feel embarrassed by all this.

Most people in whom puberty has started will answer yes to the first four questions. If the answer to the next question is no, then they have no problems; they are growing normally and are happy to be doing so.

But if the answer to 5 is yes, then you are missing out on some of the pleasure you can find in your growth.

ANOTHER STRATEGY
for growth

1. Accept all this as *normal*. The fact that penis and testicles grow means they are ready to do the work for which they are designed. It is not reasonable to expect them to grow and not to operate.

2. Remember that other people don't notice what happens to you as much as you do. The fact that you have developed a large erection is very apparent to you — but onlookers won't see it, unless you're stark naked. If you wear tight clothes then it's even less likely to be noticeable because the tightness will hold the erection down.

3. Be patient. An erection doesn't last all that long, unless you help it by thinking a lot about what you'd like to do with it. It will go in a minute or two if you let it.

4. If you wake up wet, don't try to hide the "evidence". It's nothing to be ashamed of! The sheets/pyjamas will dry in time, and the semen will just brush away. If you're really anxious about it though, make your own bed.

Check List Three

First Set
1 I am fourteen plus.
2 I am dark haired.
3 My face is beginning to be hairy.
4 I would like to shave regularly.

Second Set
1 I am eighteen plus.
2 I am fair haired.
3 I grow hardly any hair on my face.
4 I would like to shave regularly.

If you answer yes to all four of the first set, then obviously, shaving is going to be part of your life from now on (unless later you opt to grow a beard and moustache — but be warned, they aren't any easier to look after than a shaven face. Beards need trimming, shaping, shampooing. They can be as much trouble as head hair).

If you answered yes to most of the second set of questions *then you are in the majority*. Full beard growth is not established for many years — often well into the twenties or even in some cases later.

STRATEGY
for shaving

1   Look at the older men in your family. If they have strong beards, probably you will too. If not, you're likely to be smooth cheeked. Either way, settle for what you are. It's all you can do.

2   Remember that cutting hair encourages heavier and more bristly growth. Once you start shaving you'll have to go on.

3   Choose your method. A brush and safety razor? Brushless cream and cut-throat? Electric razor? Only experiment will tell you what suits you.

> 4   Shaving can increase spottiness. The cutting off of the facial hair alters the chemical balance of the skin, and may increase the risk of rash. If this happens, talk to your GP — early treatment can prevent later problems.

As for girls, there are questions boys ask at puberty about problems that worry them. As with the girls, I can't answer all of them. But here are some.

QUESTIONS Boys Ask:

Question 1   *"All round my penis I've got some white spots. I read about VD in a book, and I'm scared this is what this is, though I've never had sex."*

Answer   If you've never had intercourse then you can't have a sexually transmitted disease (see page 162). These are almost certainly the normal white-headed spots which are simply enlarged sebum glands. Sebum is the natural skin oil that lubricates the skin (in sheep it's called lanolin, and is collected to be the base of cosmetics and skin creams of all sorts). If the glands block they become bulgy with sebum and appear then as white pimples you see. Ignore them. Or, if you can't, show your doctor, who'll reassure you too.

Question 2   *"I get erections a lot, that's all perfectly normal I know, but what worries me is that my penis isn't straight when it's upright, it's got a sort of bend. It worries me — will I be able to have intercourse?"*

Answer   If this has always been there, then it's normal for you. And yes, you will be able to have intercourse. Lots of men have this sort of variation — the penis isn't as straight as a ruler. It's only if a marked bend appears in adult life and/or is accompanied by discomfort, that there might be a disorder that needs medical treatment.

Question 3   "I have breasts like a girl and they make my life hell. I can't go swimming and I can't wear tight T-shirts like other boys. Can I get an operation to get rid of them?"

Answer   Over seventy per cent of boys get some breast development during puberty. Much of this disappears by late teens and early twenties, and nothing can or need be done.

But some get so breasty that doctors agree to remove the tissue surgically. The operation leaves simple scars and the boy looks fine afterwards. Only your own doctor can help you decide whether you need this treatment or not. Meanwhile, you can go swimming — wear a loose T-shirt and tell people you get this allergy if you expose your skin to the light.

Question 4   "I have a testicle that keeps going up into my body and stays there. It will come down sometimes, but it worries me because I look so funny when I've only got one of them down."

Answer   As long as your testicle does come down, then the chances are that it will, by the time your pubertal growth is complete, come down and stay down. Check with your doctor, however, in case you need a minor operation to make sure it stays down. As for the look of it — that really need not be a worry. It *never* looks as odd to others as people think. In fact, others probably wouldn't notice if you didn't tell them.

People who have a testicle that hasn't come down at all needn't worry about their future sex life; they'll be normal lovers and fathers. And they'll be able to have sons and daughters, by the way. It's an old wives' tale that men make girl-making sperm in one testicle, and boy-making sperm in the other. However, the undescended testicle can give trouble in later life (developing diseased areas), and some surgeons today advise the removal of the undescended one at an early stage.

The reason for these problems, by the way, is the way a boy develops. The testicles start their growth in the unborn baby high inside the belly and come down to go into the scrotum at or around the time of birth. They're often quite mobile in young children, bobbing up and down from body to scrotum like a cork, and then settle into the final position at puberty.

Question 5 "*Sometimes my testicles hang very low and one hangs lower than the other. It also seems bigger than the other. Is this normal?*"

Answer Probably. The scrotum is a really rather remarkable piece of tissue. It has the job of keeping the testicles at the ideal temperature for them to do their job, which is about 95°F. The average body temperature is about 98°F so when the surrounding air is warm the scrotum relaxes and keeps the testes well away from the too hot body. But when the air is cold, then the testes are lifted by the contracting scrotum to keep them warmly tucked into the body. Elegant hydraulics which ensure the testes, which are precious and sensitive organs (as you'll know if you've ever walloped them), are well cared for.

As for the uneven size of your testicles — this too is probably normal for you. None of us, male or female, have exactly matching halves. One eye will be a slightly different size, so will one breast, so will one kidney, and so on. If you've always had one big testicle, fine. No need to worry. It's only if there is a marked change after development is complete that there may be a condition a doctor has to treat. So check with him if you're worried.

Question 6 "*I haven't been circumcised, though most of the* boys in my class at school have. Can I get this done without my parents knowing?"

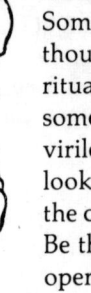

Answer The operation of circumcision is done to remove the little hood of skin that covers the tip of the penis in a newborn baby. It's done for two basic reasons — to loosen the skin if it is too tight and causing urine to be dammed back, or for ritual purposes. Some religions — Muslims and Jews — do this, though at different ages. The original reasons for ritual circumcision are forgotten now, though some people think it was to make the penis look virile at all times — and the circumcised penis looks similar to the erect penis because the glans, the cap of smooth tissue at the very tip, is exposed. Be that as it may, most doctors today feel that the operation should only be done if people have *strong* religious reasons or if they are having definite problems with a tight foreskin. It is not true, by the way, that circumcised men are "sexier" than uncircumcised.

However, if after knowing all that you still feel miserable because you are a whole man, while some of your schoolfriends have been trimmed, talk to your GP. Only he can arrange for circumcision if you need it.

In addition to the questions boys and girls ask that are specific to their gender, there are others that worry both sexes. Never forget that we're all more alike than we're different.

QUESTIONS You All Ask:

Question 1 "I'm a girl of 15 and I'm overweight — I'm five-foot-six and I weigh nine stone. My brother's too fat too, I think — he's sixteen but he doesn't worry about it, he says he never weighs himself. My mother says it's just puppy fat for both of us and won't let me diet, or make him. She says we **need** to eat bread, it's good for us. I'm sure it's bad for us — how can I diet if she won't help?"

Answer First of all, you're not too fat. People of your age and height are on the average — and these are figures collected by life insurance companies — eight stone thirteen pounds. So you're virtually spot on. As for your brother — his size is his affair, and it wouldn't be kind to make him anxious when he needn't be. The most important thing for you to do is accept that you're a normal weight for your age — and set yourself eating habits that will keep you that normal weight without any trouble for the rest of your life.

So, what is a good basic diet? Your mother's right about the need for bread; it's a useful source of protein and vitamins. If you always eat wholemeal bread — two slices a day — you'll be getting essential fibre too. Potatoes are useful as a source of vitamin C. Bread and potatoes are not in themselves fattening foods; it's what you add to them that adds the unwanted calories. Like butter, or frying, or jam. To get all the foodstuffs you need, without the empty calories — the non-nutritive, fattening ones — follow this eating plan.

Eating plan for life

Stop foods: the red ones All foods which are loaded with sugar (which provides calories but no real nutrition) should be avoided. Sweets, chocolates, biscuits, cakes, sugared breakfast cereals (even though they are vitamin enriched, they are very high in empty calories), bottled "fruit" squashes, ice cream.

Caution foods: the amber ones Some foods are high calorie but are also high in essential nutrients. So these should be used in controlled quantities. An adequate daily intake for some of them would be: bread (two slices, but wholemeal to provide fibre); fruit (an apple and orange); butter and cream (an ounce or two); potatoes (one or two small ones). Go very lightly on sweet vegetables such as corn and beetroot, but eat wholegrain cereals — like brown rice or unsweetened wholegrain breakfast cereals.

Go foods: the green ones   These are the protein foods, body-building and rich in other essential nutrients. Meat, fish, eggs, cheese. High calorie too, but there is usually a natural appetite limit to how much of them you can eat. Don't have too much fat with your meat or fish. Grilled is better than fried; plain lean meat better than, for example, commercial hamburgers. Edam is less "fatty" than other hard cheeses, cottage cheese is best of all.

Green leaf vegetables are also free because they are low calorie and high in vitamins and minerals — celery, cabbage (lovely when raw!) cucumber, fennel, watercress, lettuce, etc. Also tomatoes, peppers, mushrooms. Vegetables eaten raw, with skins on where possible, are healthier than peeled cooked ones; you get all the fibre and vitamins this way.

If you usually follow this plan, the occasional hamburger or ice cream won't do any harm. But eat that sort of fun junk food too often and you *will* get pudgy. Unless you're one of those lucky types who can eat everything there is and lick the plate and still not put on an unwanted ounce.

It helps you, whether you are naturally on the thin side, or naturally on the chubby side, to be able to control your appetite. You may feel an urge to eat when you're not really hungry — and that is the food that you don't need. Try the flowchart on pages 32—3 to understand your own eating urges.

Question 2   "*I worry a lot about eating. I'm one of a family which tends to put on weight easily, and I'd hate to get as fat as my aunty, and my mum's on the big side too. I often find I want to eat when I'm not really hungry — especially when I'm worried. Is there anything I can do not to eat too much?*"

Answer   First of all, try the algorithm — the question and answer flowchart on pages 32 and 33 — which will help you understand why you might turn to food when you're not really hungry and which will help you control your eating a little.

But, more important, you may need to understand about a tiresome illness that afflicts some people, most often girls, though it happens to boys too, and which is closely linked with eating.

It's called anorexia nervosa, or, the less well known bulimia nervosa. Anorexia means loss of appetite. So, anorexia nervosa means literally "nervous loss of appetite".

Bulimia means over-eating, so bulimia nervosa means "nervous over-eating".

Both are basically the same condition, though they seem like opposites. Actually the nerves as such aren't involved at all — only the mind. But still, the labels do explain the conditions. They mean simply that people suffering from them respond to anxiety or deep down psychological distress by changing their eating patterns.

Food is closely tied up with our emotions; animals in the wild eat only when they actually need food, but humans use food as a symbol. When a mother feeds her baby she is giving it not only calories and vitamins and other essential food; she is giving it love as well.

Religion uses food too — Catholics use bread and wine and fasting in their services, Jews and Muslims have forbidden foods as well as compulsory foods for certain times of the religious year — in fact all religions use food symbolism.

So, it's not remarkable that some people, when they become emotionally disturbed, show their anxiety as alterations in eating habits.

Those who develop the commoner anorexia nervosa become obsessed with the idea that they are fat. Everyone who looks at them can see they are anything but. They have sticklike limbs, drawn faces and look like concentration camp survivors, sometimes. Yet they still swear they are overweight

AM I REALLY HUNGRY?

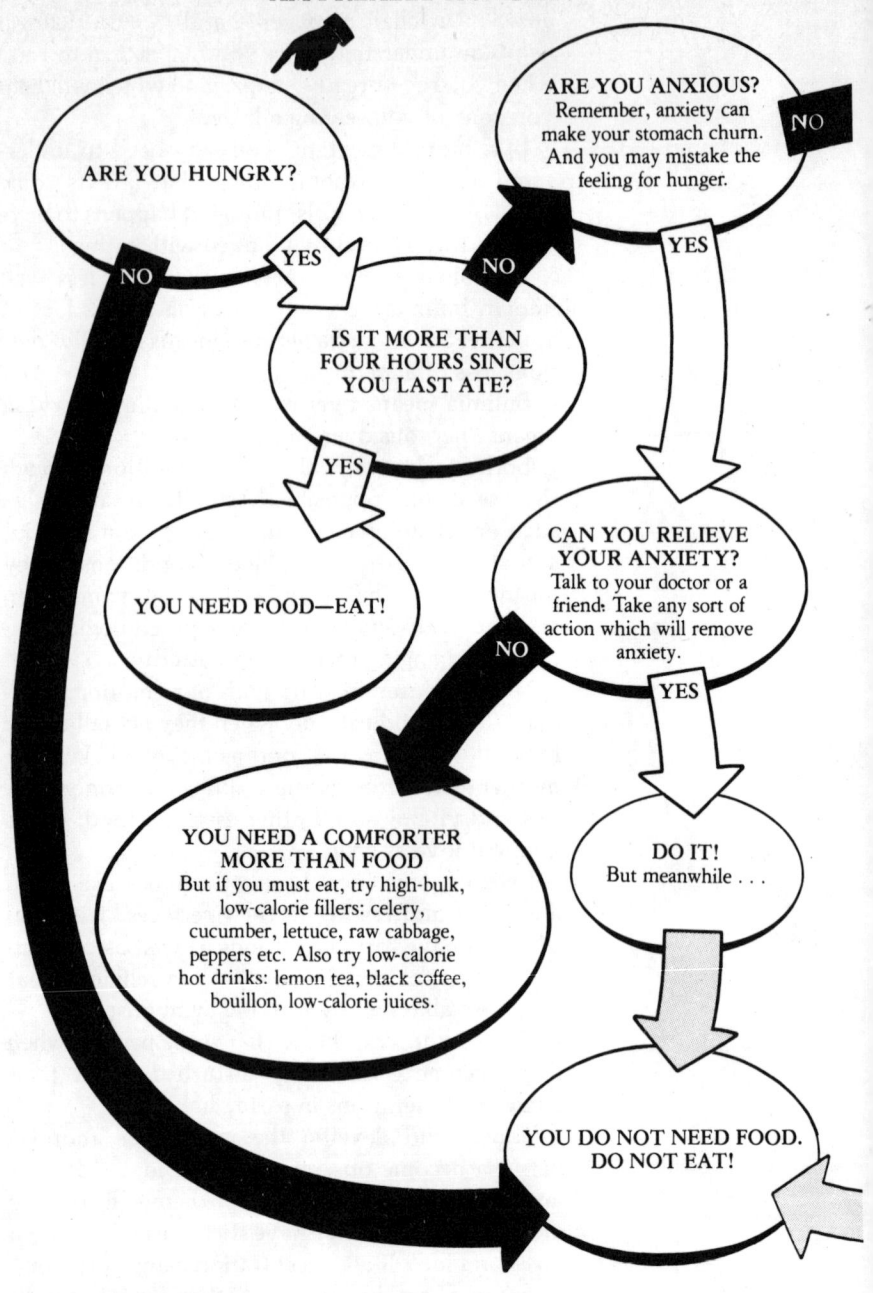

ARE YOU HUNGRY?

ARE YOU ANXIOUS?
Remember, anxiety can make your stomach churn. And you may mistake the feeling for hunger.

IS IT MORE THAN FOUR HOURS SINCE YOU LAST ATE?

YOU NEED FOOD—EAT!

CAN YOU RELIEVE YOUR ANXIETY?
Talk to your doctor or a friend. Take any sort of action which will remove anxiety.

YOU NEED A COMFORTER MORE THAN FOOD
But if you must eat, try high-bulk, low-calorie fillers: celery, cucumber, lettuce, raw cabbage, peppers etc. Also try low-calorie hot drinks: lemon tea, black coffee, bouillon, low-calorie juices.

DO IT! But meanwhile...

YOU DO NOT NEED FOOD. DO NOT EAT!

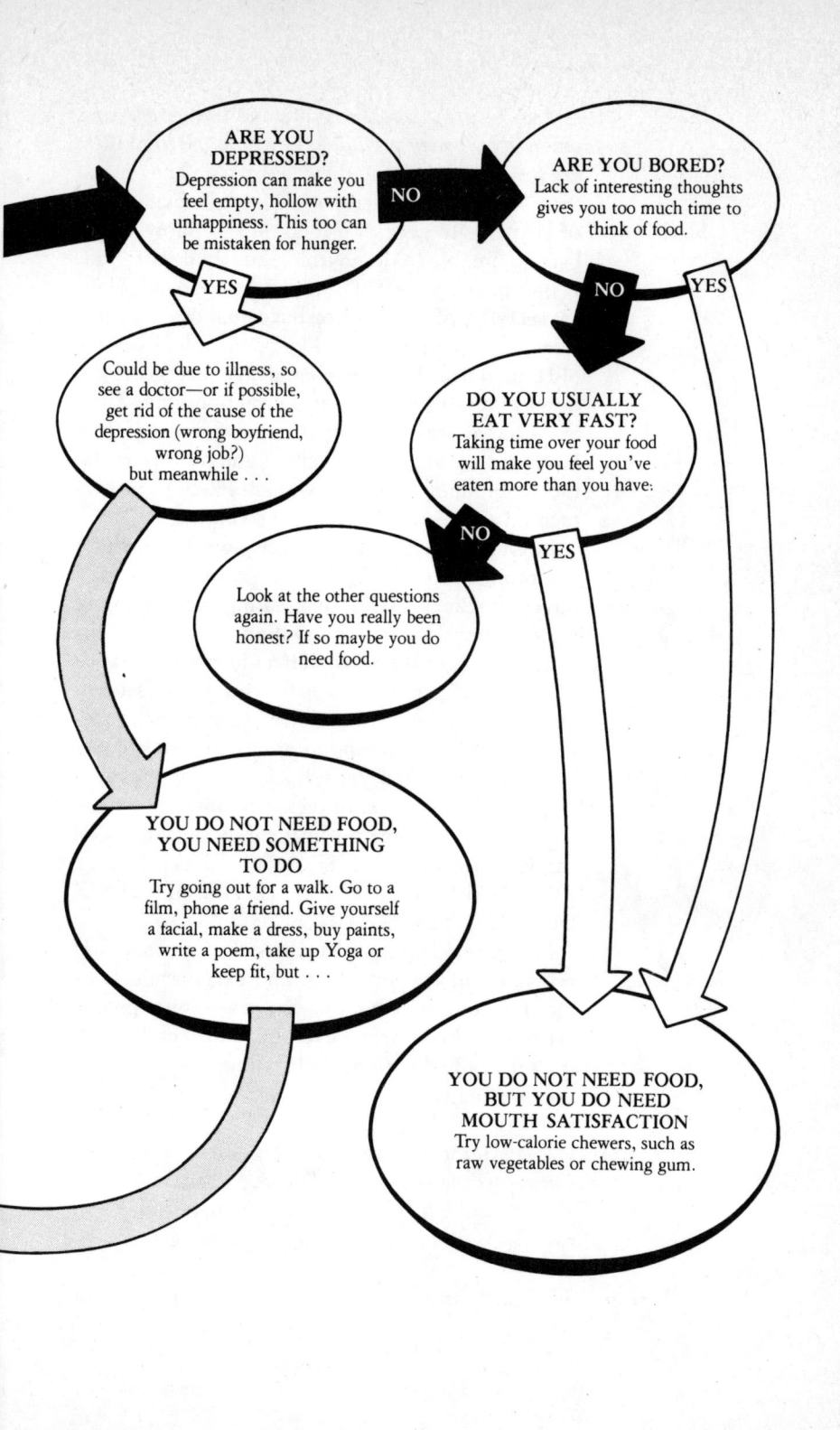

ARE YOU DEPRESSED? Depression can make you feel empty, hollow with unhappiness. This too can be mistaken for hunger.

ARE YOU BORED? Lack of interesting thoughts gives you too much time to think of food.

Could be due to illness, so see a doctor—or if possible, get rid of the cause of the depression (wrong boyfriend, wrong job?) but meanwhile...

DO YOU USUALLY EAT VERY FAST? Taking time over your food will make you feel you've eaten more than you have.

Look at the other questions again. Have you really been honest? If so maybe you do need food.

YOU DO NOT NEED FOOD, YOU NEED SOMETHING TO DO Try going out for a walk. Go to a film, phone a friend. Give yourself a facial, make a dress, buy paints, write a poem, take up Yoga or keep fit, but...

YOU DO NOT NEED FOOD, BUT YOU DO NEED MOUTH SATISFACTION Try low-calorie chewers, such as raw vegetables or chewing gum.

and go to great lengths to pretend they are eating when in fact they are not. They hide the food they are given and then say they've eaten it. They make themselves sick deliberately. They take huge doses of laxatives to get rid of food they swallow. They become unable to do anything but think of food.

Bulimia nervosa sufferers are the opposite. They eat secretly, often gobbling huge quantities of food they don't even enjoy — like bowls full of dreary old boiled rice. They are compulsive eaters who get fatter and fatter and swear they eat nothing. They are even more unhappy than anorexia sufferers because *they* at least look sweet and pitiful, unlike the fat bulimia sufferers, who are likely to be tormented and jeered at for being so big.

Interestingly, both conditions sometimes show symptoms of each other; anorexia patients may have attacks of wild over-eating, and bulimia patients periods of self-starvation.

Both sorts of illness can affect hormone balance — anorexia girls may stop having periods (they also may develop a lot of downy hair on their faces and bodies) and bulimia sufferers may also become hairy and stop their periods, though not always.

These illnesses cannot be self-treated.

They are complex medical conditions and need careful medical care. IF ANYTHING LIKE IT EVER HAPPENS TO YOU, *PLEASE* SEE YOUR DOCTOR. YOU MAY NEED HELP.

Having said all that, let me be clear and say that not all thinnish people have anorexia nervosa, nor all plumpish ones bulimia nervosa. Some people are born to be thin, some to be round. You'll know if you really have an eating illness and need a doctor's help. *Listen to yourself.*

Question 3   "*No matter what I do, I can't get into decent shape. Other people my age — I'm seventeen — look as they should but I just look like a runner bean. What exercises can I do to make me a better shape?*"

Answer   The hard answer is — none at all. If this is your

basic body type, then that's all there is to it. Almost certainly your family pattern is the same as yours — thin and wiry. It's a healthy body type to have, because all the evidence is that people like you have less heart disease, less high blood pressure, less arthritis and less strokes and heaven knows what else in later life. Not much comfort when later life couldn't matter less and you long to have a shape like an hour glass, but it's the only comfort there is. If you dress with style you can make the best of your assets — slenderness, liveliness — and then get on with living. There's no sense in fretting over what can't be changed.

Question 4 "*I get the most awful spots and blackheads on my face and chest and back and they fill up with pus and I squeeze them and they leave horrible scars. The doctor says not to eat fried food or chocolate and I'll grow out of it, but how long does he expect me to wait? There must be something more I can do.*"

Answer Yes. Spots are hell. The condition is called acne and it happens to some degree to ninety per cent of the population. So, you're by no means alone. It is usually at its worst between the ages of fourteen and seventeen, and starts to fade then, but can still leave permanent scars.

What can you do? First, don't blame yourself. It used to be said it happened because young people ate the wrong foods, were dirty and didn't wash enough, got impure sexy thoughts, and a lot of other stuff like that. *Not true.* It's a matter of heredity as much as anything — spotty parents tend to produce spotty children. It is also due to hormone action on the skin during puberty. It's very rare that diet has any effect. It's even more rare that forgetting about sex (if that were possible which happily it isn't) has any effect.

Some people find their skins clear in summer, when they tan. They are the ones who respond to ultra-violet light. A doctor can arrange for UV treatment or, in some cases, or give extra vitamin D by mouth; vitamin D being the one that is formed by the action of sunlight on the skin.

Some girls are helped by hormone treatment because it is hormonal skin changes that cause the acne in the first place. Again, a doctor can arrange this.

Others — boys as well as girls — need antibiotic treatment or special lotions or creams. These sometimes help. They sometimes don't.

The best known treatment today is skin lotion containing retinoic acid (it derives from vitamin A) used either alone or with antibiotics. Doctors claim they've given relief to eighty per cent of severe acne cases this way.

What can you do to help yourself? First, try not to squeeze zits — those yellow-headed pus-filled spots — when you get them. That tends to spread the infection and increase the scarring. Only remove the blackheads, and *don't* use your fingers; instead get a comedone extractor from the chemist and use that.

Comedone extractor

Second, nag your doctor for the help you need. If he won't give it, nag your family to change to another more sympathetic doctor. Ask to be sent to a skin specialist.

BUT once you've been seen by a good doctor, who has genuinely done all he can to help, accept the inevitable. It's something a lot of people have to live with. Remember, those pimples and scars which look to you like moon craters and volcanoes are nothing like as obvious to other people, who are far more interested, usually, in their own zits than in yours.

Question 5 *"In the last year I've been having more and more sexy dreams, and now I'm ashamed to say I get sexy thoughts before I go to sleep, and rub my body on the bed till I get a marvellous feeling. I think about having sex with people I know while I'm doing it. I'm afraid it's going to make me ill or damage me, and I keep saying to myself I won't do it, but then I do, and I feel awful about it —"*

Answer   Over the years more nonsense has been talked about this aspect of young sexual development than almost any other.

It's called masturbation, and if you look up the word in the Oxford English Dictionary you'll see it's defined as "self abuse". But it is nothing of the sort. A better and much more accurate definition would be "self-exploring" — a way of discovering and enjoying your own sexual responses by handling your own body.

Both sexes enjoy masturbation, sometimes starting very young (even babies do it) and virtually everyone does when they reach puberty. People who don't are those who have been so filled with the idea that their own sex organs are "dirty" or "disgusting" that their normal and natural responses have been frozen. Fortunately this happens less commonly these days, since sex education has come on a lot since the compilers of the Oxford English Dictionary did their work.

There are lots of ways people masturbate. Boys usually rub the penis with the fist half closed, mimicking the thrusting actions of intercourse, until the emission of semen that is the climax of sexual response. But some prefer to rub themselves against a pillow, or to rub their penis between their thighs.

Girls too differ in their ways. Some rub the clitoris, the tiny peak of sensitive tissue at the front of the surface sex organs (the vulva) until they too reach a climax, though they don't of course have an emission of semen. Others find they get their climax by pressing their legs together, or by rubbing against the bed. Whatever suits an individual is normal.

Masturbation does no harm at all. In the past people said it caused blindness, weakness, hairy growth on the palms of the hands, stammering and madness, and heaven knows what else. Well, if that were true, most of the people in the world would be blind, mad, hairy-handed stammering weaklings. Because the vast majority of people enjoy this sort of sexiness — and they *need* to. Not only is it a comfortable way to deal with sexual urges that you can't share with a partner — perhaps because you're too young to be involved in shared sex or because you don't happen to have a partner handy — it is also educational. Until you can learn how your own body works, and teach yourself to relax and enjoy personal sex, how can you expect, later on, to relax and enjoy shared sex? How can you help a partner help you, and how can you help your partner to respond comfortably if you've never had any practical experience? That is what masturbation is — the practical side of young sex education.

Question 6 "My problem is that no matter how carefully I wash, and however many different deodorants I try, I smell. I know I do — I've seen people turn away from me with their hands over their faces. It's got so bad that I don't want to go anywhere —"

Answer We all smell. There'd be something very odd about us if we didn't.

Some of the smells are very agreeable; the scent of sunwarmed clean skin is lovely.

Some are not so agreeable; the smell of unwashed armpits in which bacteria have been to work making the sweat decompose is nasty.

Some smells are very powerful communication tools; we send out scent messages to signal that we are sexually mature, and also when we're frightened and when we're ill.

These are all part of our shared inheritance with animals, but because we have developed speech, which is a very effective communication system, we tend not to be as consciously aware of scent messages as our forebears probably were.

When puberty starts, body smells change. We stop smelling like sexually immature children and start smelling like interesting sexual adults. Not all children want to grow up; for them, signs of development are frightening — and some of them are so frightened they can't even admit their fear. Instead, they try to reject what is happening to them — and may reject most particularly the normal changes of body smell that come with puberty.

None of this is conscious. The person who reacts against growing up doesn't say, "I don't want to grow up!" If he could he'd have fewer problems — talking about deep feelings makes them much easier to handle. Instead, he looks for reasons to explain his unpleasant feelings, and finds them by regarding something which is normal as something which is abnormal. He complains he smells bad, however hard he tries not to, instead of accepting that he smells like an adult person. He even imagines other people's behaviour *proves* they are right. Someone nearby uses a handkerchief because of a running nose — and the self-hating "stinker" miserably assumes it's because of him.

Of course some people *do* smell bad; the ones who don't wash, smoke like chimneys and let their hair stink like unwashed ashtrays, never clean their teeth and so on — but people like this either don't know they smell bad or don't care. If they did, they'd wash. But those who wash and perfume and deodorise and powder and scrub their teeth till their gums ache who still write desperate letters to advice columns asking for cures for their problems *never smell bad.*

What you need, if this is your problem, is not some new magic deodorant. You need help to learn to like yourself and your new adult future. You need *counselling.* [See the Information Section at the back of the book.]

Question 7 "Why is it girls are so much ahead of boys? When we were all in the junior school, we were all friends, and it was lovely. But now we're all twelve, and the boys seem so silly, and they think we're stuck up and now it's not friendly any more at all —"

Answer No one knows why it is that girls mature, generally, at a younger age than boys. But they do, and that's all there is to it. The differences between men and women continue all through life. One effect is rather sad; because boys are less mature — and this is true of emotional and social maturity as well as of physical maturity — at the age when people pair off and marry, it's usual for husbands to be older than their wives. A girl of twenty feels better matched by a boy of twenty-five, and vice versa. Which means that at the other end of life, women are far more likely to be left widows than men to be widowers; not only do the men die before their wives because they are older — they also have a shorter life span than women. But then, no one ever promised life would be fair.

All this is inevitably a very short account of something that takes a long time, from the first stirrings of the various hormones to the completion of adult development, and even after full adult characteristics have appeared there will be continuing changes. A boy of sixteen or seventeen may have his heavier muscles, his deeper voice, his hairy body and his enlarged penis and testicles — but another ten years and he'll be even more masculine to look at. The beard for example takes a number of years before it develops its full potential.

The same is true of girls. A sixteen-year-old is an adult female, but ten years from now she may be more voluptuously feminine.

So people differ in themselves as time passes — and they also differ from each other. *There is no such thing as a standard shape or size for humans.* The variations in sexual organs, in breasts, in body hair patterns, in shapes of hips, legs and chests is as wide as the variation in faces. Yet a great many people think there is one "right" shape and size for everyone, and worry themselves sick because they don't happen to fit the image. But you can see for yourself that there is no "right" one.

What were you born to be?

Another factor which has a great deal of effect on the finished physical adult you will be is not so much the changes of puberty as your basic body type.

Almost fifty years ago an American scientist classified people into three main body types. *He did not suggest that there were only three*

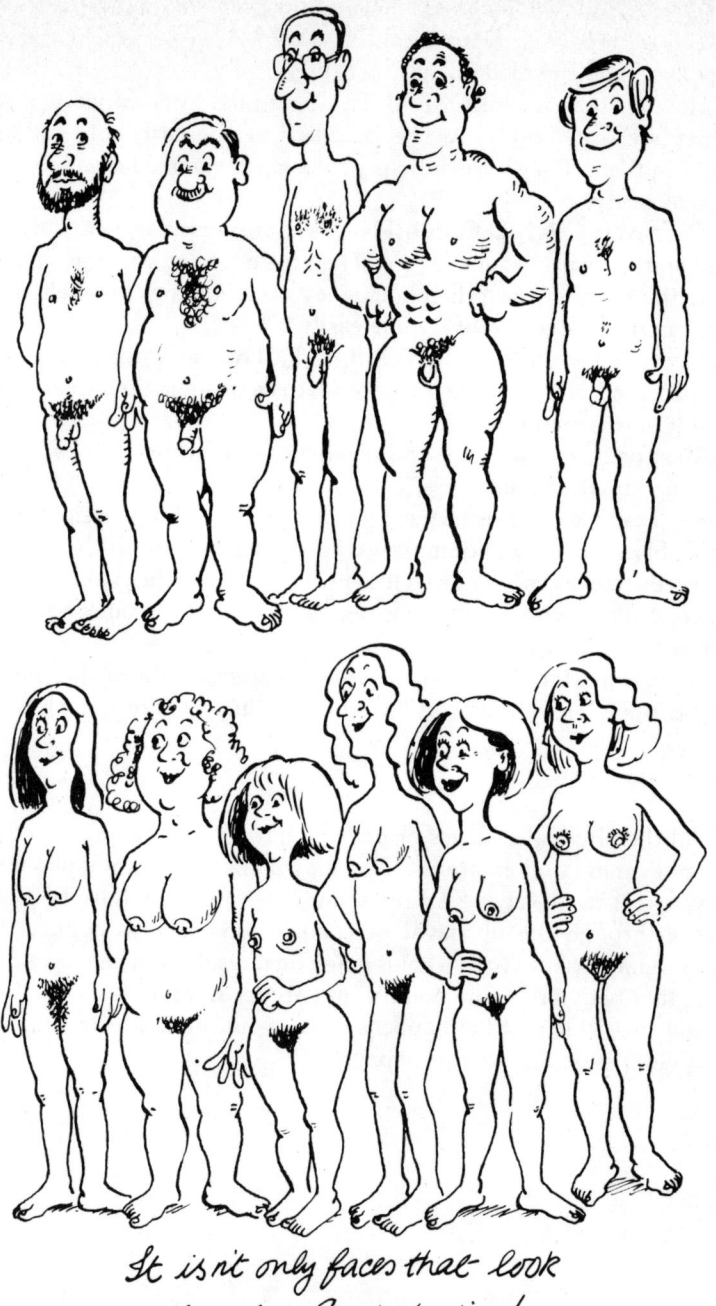

It isn't only faces that look different — So do bodies!

kinds of people in the world. The point he made was that there were three basic types which go to make up the finished person, and that each type could be included in varying degrees.

The first type is ENDOMORPH. These tend to be round and soft, with quite a lot of body fat. They are likely to have curly hair, and small teeth and ears. They have difficulty in losing unwanted fat and get overweight easily.

The next type is MESOMORPH. These are muscular, with very little body fat; long armed and legged. Their teeth tend to be large, and they have thick but fairly straight hair. They gain fat if they are underactive but can usually get rid of it quite easily.

The remaining type is ECTOMORPH. Long and thin, with rather spindly arms and legs. Their hair tends to be straight. And they usually find it hard to put on weight.

Most people show some characteristics of all three groups, though one may predominate.

For example, a shot putter who needs heavy body weight would probably be mainly endomorph with some mesomorph thrown in — he needs to be muscular as well as heavy. On the other hand, a female ballet dancer who needs long legs and lightness would be mainly ectomorph. And so on.

It can help a lot to understand these somatypes, because then you can avoid pursuing activities as careers for which you're not physically suited.

All the physical changes of puberty have a very strong effect on a person's mind and emotions. This may seem a very obvious thing to say, but it needs saying all the same. Even people whose bodies are going through the upheaval of change don't always connect their emotional anxieties with what is going on physically. They develop the idea that body and mind and feelings are separate things.

But they aren't. What happens inside your mind affects your body and vice versa. So, what *is* happening?

CHAPTER TWO
YOU AND YOUR PERSONALITY

Hormones are happening. These chemical messengers which prod various body organs into growing, changing, developing new functions, act on the brain too since of course it is part of the body. And though no one yet has been able to point to a portion of the brain and say, "This is where the mind is," or, "This is where feelings come from," the brain as a whole is known to be the source of these. So, what affects the brain affects mind and feelings.

Unfortunately, the changes that happen in mind and feelings are unlike the changes which happen to other body structures, in one important way. *They are not permanent.* Breasts once grown don't disappear, a penis once developed doesn't shrink back to baby size. But aspects of mind and emotions and personality — which is the sum of all the different aspects of you — can and do change bewilderingly in all directions, going backwards as well as forwards. The emotional maturity you were sure you had at fifteen seems to have vanished a year later; the self confidence with which you were brimming at twelve abandons you by the time you're half way through middle school and need it most desperately.

Because no one yet has been able to define accurately where mind and emotions and personality are situated inside you, it's very difficult to describe them. But it is possible to identify the various threads that go to make up the different strands. Let's start with *emotions*.

These are the feelings of love, hate, anger, fear, joy, despair that are so familiar; after all, we have them from the moment we're born (maybe before!). We take our own emotional face as much for granted as we do our physical face; what we are as we start puberty is what we've always been.

But puberty affects our emotions profoundly, just as it changes us physically. Indeed the physical changes themselves create some of the emotional ones. Take the matter of the difference in size that comes at this stage. This is most obvious in boys — they, remember, can grow as many as four or five inches in as many months — but it happens to girls too, and it's very disconcerting to find you take up more of the world's cubic air space than you used to.

Which can make you clumsy. Falling over your feet is a natural thing to do when you've gone up two shoe sizes in just one school term or so. And clumsiness makes you self-conscious and irritable, especially when other people make nasty remarks about it.

And there's another complication. The changes in your physical body are largely connected with the development of adult sexual characteristics. Your new body equipment is designed for the making of new human beings. Your new body smell is designed to help you attract a sexual partner in order that you can make new human beings. Your new appearance matters hugely because it adds to the attractiveness of your smell to draw the sexual partner you need with whom to make — you get the picture.

All of which means that you are, as you move on into puberty, flooded with very intense sexual feelings.

You've been finding pleasure in the messages your senses can give you ever since you were a baby. Nuzzling into soft skin the way a baby nuzzles into his mother when he breastfeeds is a very sensual experience. Curling up in a mother's arms when you're sleepy is a very sensual experience for a toddler. And from infancy on, you've handled your own body because you like the feelings you get from doing so. Virtually every boy falls asleep holding his genitals in one hand, just as virtually all small girls like to tuck one hand over their genitals when they go to sleep. (How do I know? By being a nurse in adults' wards as well as children's wards. Believe me, everyone does it!)

All this is sexual, of course, and most people realise that. But not all the new feelings of puberty are recognised as being sexy ones.

Some people become very aggressive. This is very likely to happen to boys because they have this sudden upsurge of new strength and they have to try it out. And of course people expect boys to be tough and rough, and in a sense, allow it, where they frown on aggressive girls.

Some people become dreamy and withdrawn. To sit and listen to the words of pop songs or poetry, to lie on your back in the woods and stare up at the sky and feel so miserable that you just lie and cry till your ears are full of tears for no reason you can put words to, is sexual behaviour — a rehearsal for the powerful experience of sexual involvement that will come in the future. This happens to both sexes.

Some people become very sociable, and spend a lot of time organizing mixed parties and outings and shared activities for a lot of friends.

They work like beavers at making sure everyone has got something interesting to do and somewhere interesting to go and someone interesting to be with on their nights out. They get very miserable if they can't make and carry through their plans. This is sexual behaviour too, a pattern of personal partner seeking, but disguised (a little) as helping others.

Most people get moody. They swing from high elation to utter gloom and back again. One minute the world's their own possession, and the next they wouldn't take it gift-wrapped with discount stamps. They feel confused by their own changeability — no wonder everyone around them gets confused too.

Something people don't always realise is that it is themselves who are changing. They feel as though they are the same as they always were, but that outsiders are behaving differently. The Mum and Dad who used to be affectionate and gentle suddenly become tough and complaining and lacking in understanding. The friends who were once fun to be with become spiteful and snotty, the life that once was interesting and worthwhile becomes dull and dreary. Home stops being a haven and starts feeling like a trap.

It is true that some of the changes that you recognise are coming from outsiders. Parents *do* change as their children grow up, and do show different behaviour to a person when he's a baby and when he's a child and very much so when he's starting to be a new adult. Friends change, just as you do, and their pubertal experiences affect the way they act towards you. But a lot of the change you experience is happening *inside you* and unless you understand and accept that, you'll never get your life sorted out the way you want it.

So, always remember, whenever you find yourself thinking, "I'm having a lot of trouble with — my parents/friends/teachers/whoever," always to add, *"so they're having a lot of trouble with me."*

STRATEGY
for coping with emotional change

1   Think about whether you are having emotional problems at all. If you are not — you

just feel a bit fed up sometimes — go no further. There is no need to do anything about something that is not all that much of a problem.

2   Write down what your problems are. For example, something like this:
I am depressed quite often.
I keep on having arguments with my friend(s).
I keep on having arguments with my parents. Etcetera.

3   Look at the problems which involve other people, and make a list of the things that you know have affected them recently. For example, something like this:
My friend's parents are getting divorced.
My friend has failed O levels/CSEs, etc.
My father has recently changed his job/lost his job. Etcetera.

If necessary make discreet enquiries about what might be upsetting the people in your life, if you can't see any obvious reasons for any changes in them. Casual conversation directed at what the *other* person thinks and feels, rather than about what you're thinking and feeling can tell you a lot.

4   If you can find changes in other people that are causing the problems you are having, then there is nothing you can do about the problems. It is the other person who must make the effort to change the situation between you — you are powerless.

5   You have now identified which of your problems are due to changes in *you*. Now make

your last list — this time of the things that have changed in your life apart from the changes of puberty. For example, something like this:

I have not done as well at school as I wanted to.

I have recently moved from one home to another.

I have recently had an illness.

Etcetera.

6 *Be both kind to yourself, and firm with yourself.*

A) If you're unsettled because you've recently moved home, for example, then you need to give yourself time to get used to your new situation. Depression and anxiety will slowly ease — but trying to rush the process will only make them worse. When a mood of misery hits you, *give yourself a treat*. Maybe a new record, or something to wear if you can afford it. If you can't because you've no money, then it's rough — but if you try you'll think of *something* that will make you feel less aware of your depression.

B) If there is no obvious cause for your feelings, then be firm with yourself, and refuse to give in to them. It's very easy to crawl into a corner on your own and wallow in your misery — but that makes the misery last longer. Taking a deep breath and forcing yourself to get out and be polite and nice to people will help you actually feel polite and nice.

C) Help your friends/parents, etcetera, to help you by telling them honestly that you don't enjoy the rows and miseries and depression that hit you any more than they do, but

> that it just seems to happen. Ask them to be patient when you have a bad patch. *And do the same for them when they need help.*
>
> D) If your friends/parents can't give you the help you feel you need to talk about your worries, then look for someone else. Maybe a teacher or counsellor at school; maybe your friend's mum; maybe a neighbour. There's usually someone you could trust to be helpful, if you look around you.

This strategy is a basic one, designed to help you avoid making minor problems worse by failing to accept and tolerate the inevitable mood swings that come with puberty, but it will also help you deal with specific arguments. So will the flowchart opposite.

Personality

Even more important than the ways in which emotions change at puberty are the differences we all have in our *personalities*. I've already shown that we can have different emotional profiles — but we're more than emotions and hormones and bodies, of course. There is that almost indefinable quality of *self* that is labelled personality.

Understanding your own personality is about the hardest thing there is to do. You live inside it, so you can't see it any more than you can see your own eyes without looking in a mirror. But let's have a go —

Often personality is most clearly identified by behaviour.

If you look at a row of people standing at attention, and all wearing the same clothes — say a platoon of soldiers — you can't possibly say what sort of people they are. All you can know is that they're all men, and they're all soldiers.

But see them out of uniform and hear them talking, watch them moving, see them doing what they want to do, and you begin to get some knowledge of their differing personalities. That one's a quiet type; that one's a chatterer; that one's a cheerful optimistic person; that one's a nervous pessimist; and so on.

And if the people you're looking at are both men and women, you're likely to add on a few other judgements about personality. That quiet one is very feminine, that aggressive strong one is very masculine.

HOW TO HAVE AN ARGUMENT

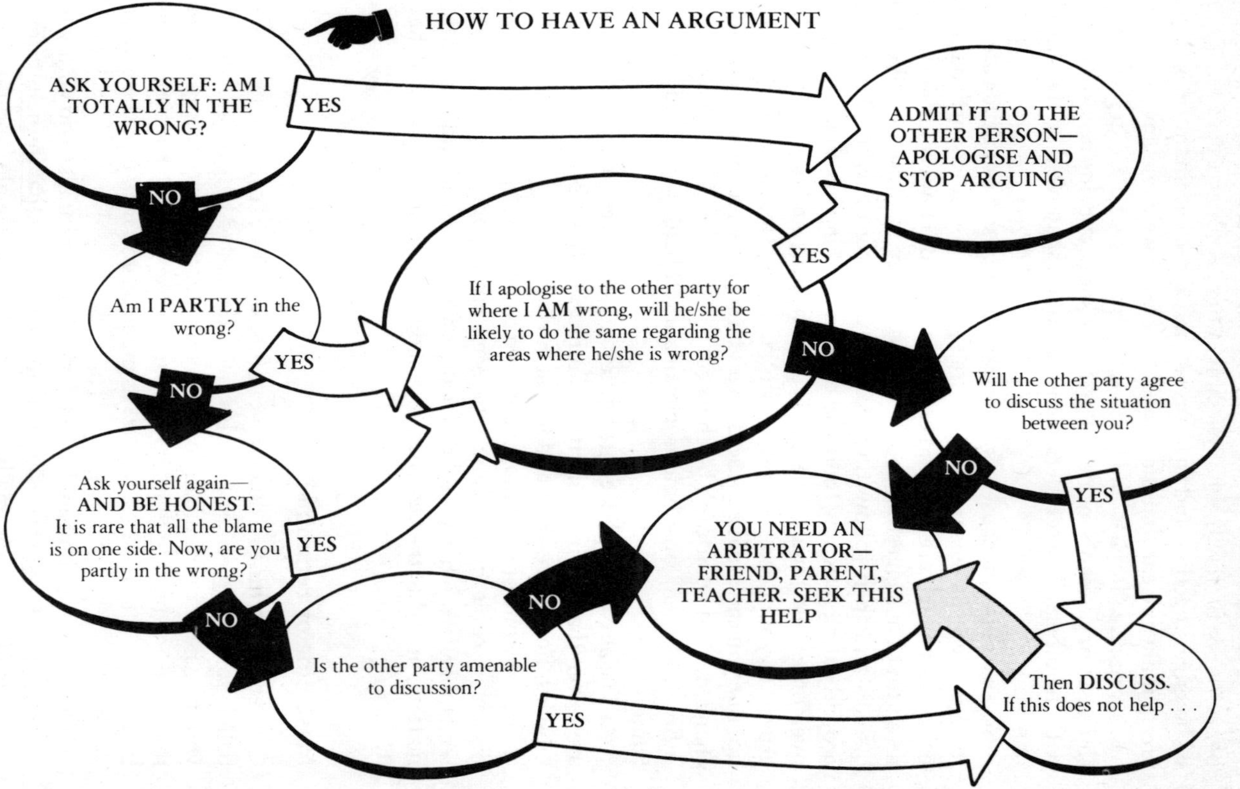

ASK YOURSELF: AM I TOTALLY IN THE WRONG?
YES
ADMIT IT TO THE OTHER PERSON— APOLOGISE AND STOP ARGUING
NO
Am I PARTLY in the wrong?
YES
NO
Ask yourself again— AND BE HONEST. It is rare that all the blame is on one side. Now, are you partly in the wrong?
YES
NO
If I apologise to the other party for where I AM wrong, will he/she be likely to do the same regarding the areas where he/she is wrong?
YES
NO
Will the other party agree to discuss the situation between you?
NO
YES
Is the other party amenable to discussion?
NO
YES
YOU NEED AN ARBITRATOR— FRIEND, PARENT, TEACHER. SEEK THIS HELP
Then DISCUSS. If this does not help . . .

This information, however, isn't enough to tell you what the people you're looking at are really like, because we all tend to change our behaviour to fit in with what we think other people expect of us. If a lot of boys get together and the noisiest and most dominant ones in the group make it clear that the only sort of boys welcome amongst them are aggressive "boyish" individuals, then those who are in fact rather shy and unaggressive inside will put on a show of being boyish to fit in with the others. The real personality becomes shadowed by the surface one.

So, one of the most useful of all strategies is to sort out which ideas of the many you have learned so far are right for you, and worth hanging on to; and which are not, and can be jettisoned. However, this doesn't mean that I'm suggesting people should simply identify their likes and dislikes and then follow them slavishly. A person who likes sitting around eating fattening food and dislikes working has to learn how to overcome these things if he/she is to be healthy and happy. Changing aspects of your behaviour is an essential strategy for successful growing up. But you can't make those changes until you know what needs to be changed. And what can't be changed.

So, first then, an obvious personality thread — masculinity and femininity.

As I've already explained, the differences between males and females are fewer than their similarities. Both sexes have brains, both have muscles, both have arms and legs at each corner.

Even the bits of us that are supposed to be the most different — sex organs — come in matching sets. Men have nipples on their chests, remember. It's what each gender does with its basic equipment that matters, not what the basic equipment does to the individuals who have it.

Masculine or Feminine?

Gender has nothing to do with your interests (boys can be interested in ballet, for example, just as girls can be interested in football), though you may have been taught to enjoy some activities according to what the adults in your life think is right for your sex. It may have something to do with your abilities, but not as much as you may have been led to believe.

But this does not mean that gender has nothing at all to do with your behaviour and reactions. There's evidence to show that the male human is in some ways emotionally different from the female, and that these differences are based on the different hormones each gender has. The male hormone testosterone does more than make a man able to father babies. It also may make him rather more sexy and aggressive, rather less dependent, rather more ambitious. The female hormones oestrogen and progesterone don't just work at taking a pregnancy through from egg to infant; they may make a girl rather more protective, rather more dependent on others, rather less pushing.

However, there are people of strong political views who get very angry indeed at any suggestion that men and women are different in this way. They say that *all* the differences are learned behaviour, and that women have been made dependent, men aggressive, by the way they are treated in childhood and that it's high time we changed all that and started rearing boys and girls as people rather than merely men and women.

Either way, the fact remains that at present there are some forms of human behaviour that are regarded by most people as being "typically feminine" and "typically masculine". And a girl who finds she has "male" traits can feel very bothered, just as a boy who finds he has "female" ones can get panicky.

But this is daft — because we all have a mixture of responses and tastes and needs. Every man in the world has some "feminine" traits; every woman who ever breathed has some "masculine" ones. Understanding which you've got of each can be useful. An important life strategy is making the best of the traits you have — and you can't do that till you know what they are. So, a questionnaire.

To use this questionnaire take a sheet of paper, and list your answer A, B, C, or D — and you can give more than one answer to every question, if you need to.

Masculinity/Femininity Index

Question 1   When I buy new clothes

    A. I am very fussy, and try on several things in lots of different shops before I decide.

    B. Couldn't care less about what clothes look like — just want them to be comfortable, and buy whatever fits.

    C. Take lots of time buying special gear like sports clothes, but don't care about ordinary clothes.

Question 2   Before I go out of the house

    A. I take plenty of time to make sure I'm tidy, that I'm clean and I smell nice.

B. Couldn't care less about what I look like — and have to be nagged to take a bath.

C. Take trouble about how I look for a special date, but usually don't bother.

Question 3   My own room (or share of room)

A. Usually looks tidy.

B. Usually looks like a tip.

C. Is left to my mother to deal with.

Question 4   If I saw people I knew involved in an argument and getting really angry with each other — looking as though they were going to hit each other

A. I would get well away from them, and let them sort it out for themselves.

B. Get excited and go and join in, maybe taking sides.

C. Think it looked fun to go and watch and cheer them on.

D. Try to separate them.

Question 5   If I heard someone I knew had been spreading untrue stories about me

A. I would pretend I hadn't been told and ignore the whole business.

B. I would go and find the person and start a row about the stories.

C. I would go and find out if I'd been told the truth.

D. I would tell false stories about the other person as a retaliation.

Question 6   If a person was unkind to me in front of other people

A. I would want to cry.

B. I would get very angry but be too angry to say anything.

C. I would get very angry but be able to be very rude back.

D. I'd hit the person hard.

Question 7   If I thought I'd been cheated in a shop

A. I'd let them get away with it, rather than start a row.

You and Your Personality 53

    B. I'd complain at once and insist on getting my money back.
    C. I'd say nothing in the shop, but go home and write a strong letter of complaint to the manager.
    D. I'd get my parents to sort it out.

Question 8   *If I saw a child crying in the street, looking lost*
    A. I'd leave the child alone, seeing no reason to get involved.
    B. Talk to him/her to see what the trouble was and try to help.
    C. Look around for someone else to take care of the child.

Question 9   *If I saw a big child hitting a smaller child in the street*
    A. I'd leave them to sort it out for themselves.
    B. I'd separate them at once.

Question 10   *If I heard a bus conductor being rude to another passenger because of his race or nationality*
    A. I wouldn't say anything.
    B. I'd tell the conductor to shut up.
    C. I'd talk loudly to another person on the bus about the conductor's behaviour, in the hope that another person would confront the man.

Question 11   *If two of my friends had a row with each other*
    A. I'd keep out of it and not care what they did.
    B. I'd go to each one separately and try to persuade them to make it up.
    C. I'd say nothing but hope they'd made it up again.

Question 12   *The person who usually looks after the house and does the cooking takes a part time job. So,*
    A. I take it for granted that nothing will change at home.
    B. I take it for granted I will do more housework and shopping and cooking etc. from now on.
    C. I take it for granted someone else in the household will do more housework and shopping and cooking from now on.

Question 13   *When I think about my future the most important thing is*

A. The job I will have.
B. The person I will marry.
C. I don't think about it at all.

Question 14   I think that to be really happy in life

A. I will need to be successful and have a lot of money.
B. I will need to have a lot of friends.
C. I don't know.

Question 15   When I think about the future

A. I take it for granted I will have children.
B. I take it for granted I won't have children.
C. I don't care either way.

Question 16   When I listen to popular music

A. It's the meaning of the words of the song that matters.
B. It's the beat of the music that matters.
C. It's a mixture of both that matters.

Question 17   Romantic love stongs

A. Usually make me cry.
B. Never make me cry.
C. Sometimes make me feel like crying.

Question 18   When people talk about love

A. I like to join in.
B. I think it's sentimental and silly.
C. Sometimes I join in, sometimes I don't.

Question 19   I think other people's love stories are

A. Always very interesting.
B. Always very boring.
C. Interesting only if you know the people involved.

Question 20   I most enjoy

A. Being with boys.

B. Being with girls.
C. Being with both boys and girls.
D. Being on my own.

Analysis

Questions 1 and 2: These measure attitudes to *appearance*. Never think only girls care about how they look, however. Boys care just as much but don't always feel they can admit it; among some boys it's said to be "cissy" to be interested in cleanliness and smartness, so those who are will hide the fact. So, whatever you answered to these two questions makes no difference to your masculinity/femininity index. Clean or dirty, smart or scruffy, you're right for the gender you are.

Question 3: This shows not whether you're masculine or feminine, but whether you were born with a taste for *order* (which can happen to either sex) or whether you've learned to be tidy/messy. People who give answer C show nothing special about their gender identity — but do show they've got daft mothers who spoil them!

Question 4: This measures *aggressiveness*. The classic feminine response would be A because femininity is often thought to be passive. The classic masculine response would be B or C because males are expected to enjoy aggressiveness. *However* if you answered with D you could either be behaving in a very brave feminine way in hating violence and having the courage to try to end it — or in a very masculine way in, again, hating violence and being prepared to try to end it.

Question 5: This is another measure of *aggressiveness* but of the more subtle sort. Answer A is classically feminine, in that it avoids direct confrontation; answer B is classically masculine in that it relishes confrontation; answer C is the most sensible response for either males or females — and answer D is just nasty, whatever the sex of the person who gave it.

Question 6: This measures the way people handle *aggression directed at them* and the answers aren't as obvious as you might think. Answer A may seem classically feminine — but can be very masculine because both genders can need to cry. *Actually* crying is different, of course; girls are allowed to, boys are jeered at. D may seem classically masculine, but it can be feminine because both genders can be short tempered. Answers B and C are also ambiguous; males are less verbal than females so may be unable to express anger in words — but females are often taught to bite back their anger.

Question 7: This measures attitudes to *justice* and these are neither masculine nor feminine, though answer C is the most feminine response in that it deals with the injustice but avoids head-on confrontation (i.e. aggressiveness). Answer D could be given by either gender; it is the response of someone not yet mature enough to handle his/her own injustices.

Questions 8, 9, 10, and 11: These four questions measure *compassion* and *concern for others*. The obvious masculine answers are A, the obvious feminine answers B, the obvious very young person's answers are C. But don't be misled. It can be very masculine to be protective of the helpless. So either gender could give answer B. And the C answers? They are those of people who feel a desire to care, but who don't want to get involved — and that could be either girls who have been taught to be passive, or boys who have been taught it's cissy to show they care.

An important point here: Very strongly masculine people — those who have the courage to do as they think is right, no matter what other males think of them — could give all B answers, the feminine ones. It takes a strong caring person to look after a lost child, stand up to a bully and try to reconcile fighters. So really these questions measure humanity, more than gender differences.

Question 12: This measures stereotyped attitudes to *domesticity*. The obvious masculine answer is A or C. The obvious feminine answer is B. These are not necessarily the *right* answers for each gender, however. In a sensible modern household, both genders would, it is hoped, answer B.

Questions 13 and 14: These both measure *ambition*. The obvious masculine answers are A, the obvious feminine answers are B and the obvious very young answers are C. Fortunately with more adult awareness of the need to treat both boys and girls as individuals rather than as sexual stereotypes, fewer young people today will have given the obvious answers. The people most likely to have got it right are those who gave both A and B answers to question 13 and B to question 14.

Question 15: This is a total cheat. It is *not* true that girls care more than boys about having children. Both sexes care — but maybe girls find it easier to admit it.

Questions 16, 17, 18 and 19: These questions deal with *emotional attitudes*. The obvious feminine responses are answers A, and the obvious masculine responses are B. Really mature people who are a smooth mixture of both genders (as the most happy successful people in the world are) will give C as their answers.

Question 20: Another cheat to end with. You may think the obvious stereotyped feminine answer is *A* — but it is also the obvious stereotyped male response, since very "macho" men are uneasy in the company of women (except for sexual purposes) and are happier to be "one of the boys". Age actually matters more than gender here; very young people often feel more comfortable in the company of their own sex. It takes maturity and wisdom to give the best answer, which is *C*.

Introvert or Extrovert

We can now — thank heavens — leave gender and concentrate on those personality pieces that belong to both sexes.

An important one is that which is labelled *introvert* or *extrovert*. In common language an introvert is someone who looks inwards towards himself, and an extrovert is someone who looks outwards to other people. But as with the male/female differences, no one is ever totally one or the other. Introverts will have their extrovert moments and vice versa.

Let's take a look at a couple of extreme characters — one introvert, one extrovert — just to see the difference between them.

Introvert	*Extrovert*
A quiet person.	Very lively and talkative.
Spends much of his/her time alone, probably daydreams a lot.	Usually with a crowd, full of ideas for fun and games.
Doesn't mix at parties.	Always the life and soul of parties.
Has few friends, and tends to keep them a long time.	Makes friends easily, and drops them just as fast.
Won't push him/herself forward at school or work.	Never afraid to make a fool of him/herself, or to take a lead.
Never volunteers for anything.	Always willing to have a go.
Rarely displays anger but can bear a grudge for years.	Shows anger when he/she feels it, but doesn't bear grudges.
Tends to wear quiet clothes.	Wears clothes that stand out, whether they are smart or scruffy.
Will choose a career where he/she can work alone.	Will go for a job where there are lots of people around.

Both of these descriptions are of extremes. In practice, though there are some people who fit these extremes, these are far more in the middle ground, a mixture of both. And being a mixture of both is clearly ideal, since that will mean you're a well-balanced person, and will have fewer problems than the extreme types will. Also, of course, either men or women can be of either type.

Your own balance

This questionnaire will help you work out what your balance is. Answer each question with a yes or no.

Yes scores 4; usually but not always scores 3; half and half — sometimes yes, sometimes no — scores 2; sometimes but not usually scores 1; and no scores *nil*. Your own judgement will show you what the numerical value per question should be.

Questionnaire

1. I care a lot about the way I look — I take a lot of trouble over clothes and make-up.
2. I like being with a lot of people.
3. I'd rather go to something I don't like such as a wrestling match with a lot of people than to something I do, such as a good film, on my own.
4. I hate being on my own. Solitude makes me really miserable and bored.
5. I get on well with strangers — mix in with everyone and anyone.
6. I have a big list of names and addresses and phone numbers in my contact book.
7. If I see someone in difficulty on the street — looking at a map, say, or fallen over or dropping their shopping, I offer to help.
8. When people at school/work need someone to take charge I'm always glad to do it. I like responsibility.
9. I prefer to work or act as one of a team rather than on my own, though I like to be the leader of it.
10. I make up my mind quickly — I'm good at decisions.
11. I am easily persuaded to change my mind by someone who gives me good reasons to do so. I am open to suggestion.
12. I am always ready to take the middle road in an argument — I prefer compromise.

13 When I'm wrong, I'm not afraid to say so. I apologise willingly.
14 If something makes me angry, I'm not afraid to make a fuss about it. I have made scenes in public places like shops or restaurants.
15 When I'm with friends in a restaurant or other public place and notice other people are listening to what I'm saying, I like it. I often talk loudly so that people *can* overhear.
16 I would rather talk than listen.
17 I would rather be told facts than theories.
18 I think mysticism, like fortune telling, etcetera, is rubbish.
19 I admire people who are brave and confident. Cautious people irritate me.
20 When I am upset or worried about something I am able to push it out of my mind. I do not brood.
21 I like standing up in class or at work to speak or put on an act.
22 I would be willing to stand up and speak elsewhere among strangers — at a public meeting for example.
23 I am not afraid of "making a fool of myself". I'd rather take chances like that than just be anonymous.
24 I'd jump at the chance of appearing on TV.
25 I think talking or thinking about getting old and dying is morbid and boring.

Check your score. If it is a hundred then you are completely extrovert.

If you score nil, then you are a complete introvert.

If you score between forty and sixty then you are well balanced.

If you score between sixty and eighty you are quite extrovert, but able to be happy in your own company, and are reasonably thoughtful about others.

If you score between twenty and forty then you are quite introvert, but can come out and mix with others.

Only you can judge whether or not you need to make any efforts to change yourself — and people *can* change their behaviour, even though the basic introvert/extrovert pattern is probably an inborn part of your personality. That of course is what skilful adult living is about — changing the way you behave, even though you can't change the way you feel.

You judge in two ways: by considering your score, and by thinking *honestly* about the way other people relate to you. If you score eighty plus, you may discover, if you're really honest, that you steamroller some people, make them feel inadequate and put upon.

If you score twenty down, you may realise that you make other people uneasy by your quietness and embarrassed by your standoffishness.

You might say that as long as you're happy yourself, to hell with how other people feel about you; and up to a point that's true. People who fret all the time about what others think of them, and who constantly struggle to make themselves over into a new image to please onlookers make themselves very miserable indeed — and never succeed in pleasing everyone, anyway. But there is a happy balance to be found — and if you discover that you upset more people than you make comfortable by your behaviour, then there is a case for modifying aspects of it. You don't have to change yourself completely; it's not necessary even if it could be done. Just *modify*.

STRATEGY
for an introvert

1   Take a look at your family situation. Do your parents tend to encourage your introvert behaviour and like you to stay safely at home?

2   If the answer to Question 1 is yes, then talk to your parents. Tell them that you are concerned about your aloofness from other people and intend to change. Show them this strategy — see if they will help you with it. If they say yes, fine — but make it clear that you want to be in charge of it.

    If they say no, never mind. You can do it on your own.

3   Collect the names, addresses and phone numbers of all the people you know and like the look of at school/work. Try not to be put off by the extroverts. They may be noisy, but you need them — and once you get to know them they may not be as dislikeable as you think.

4   Join something. *Anything*. School or work societies and social groups. Outside clubs (get a list from the local library or the Citizens' Advice Bureau — their address is available at the Post Office. Also see p. 193–6.) Whatever you are interested in, somewhere there will be a club for people who are of like mind. *Find them.*

5   Invite four or five of your new contacts round to your house one evening. And *invite at least one extrovert*. He/she will help you cope when the conversation lags.

    If your parents can't or won't co-operate, this stage is undoubtedly difficult. In fact, it's impossible. You'll have to do without it and work harder at getting the most out of the contacts you make at school/work/clubs. Join in when people go off to a movie or for a meal somewhere. If they don't, suggest they do — "Let's all go get a hamburger" isn't too difficult to say.

6   When you're invited to something by one of your new contacts (and you will be) *accept*. It's too easy to say no. In fact, tell yourself you'll accept everything and anything that comes your way for the next month, even things you don't expect to like. Later on, when you've got into the habit of accepting, you can start to be more selective — because

then you'll be selecting on the basis of interest, not introversion.

7   Make yourself an out-and-about pattern for the week. If you know you've got to go bowling on Monday, folk club on Wednesday and swimming on Friday, you give yourself less chance to sit alone in your room.

8   Stick to your new plan for a minimum of six months. Then look at your social life and your friendships, and assess your progress. If you are still tending to spend too much time alone contemplating your own belly button, then go back to step four and *start again*.

10 Be kind to yourself. If after a second try, you're still miserable being with other people, allow yourself to stop trying. At the very least you should have a couple more friends than you used to have — and that is great.

This strategy will not convert you into an extrovert. It should, however, make you into a more sociable and rather more comfortable introvert.

STRATEGY
for an extrovert

1   Assess your home situation. Are you all bouncy outgoing cheerful people? (Get the rest of the family to do the questionnaire.)

2   If the answer is yes, it is possible that your extrovert behaviour is learned rather than inbred for you. Take another look at the

questionnaire, and check whether you answered on the basis of your *real* feelings, or on the basis of what you actually do, and learned to do from your family. If your score comes out nearer introversion this time, then you don't need this strategy. You're already as balanced as you can be.

3   If the answer to Question 1 is no, then your extroversion is part of you. Now, take a look at the people at school/work. Do you feel they like you? Or do some of them get irritated because you overwhelm them? If you can honestly answer no, stop here. You're coping well, offending no one, and need not change anything.

4   If the answer to Question 3 was yes, think about *why*. Make a list of the things you think one of the people who gets irritated with you would write down, if asked to describe you. "Noisy!" "Pushy!" "Know All!" "Big headed!" "Nosy!" would be a typical list. (*Do not ask others* to make this list for you. It's self-assessment that is the key to this strategy.)

5   Work on just *one* of the things on the list. For example, next time you're in a crowd, bite your tongue sometimes to let other people talk. *Make* yourself listen. *You do not have to stop talking altogether*. This is a modifying strategy, not a change-over one.

6   Work on the other items on the list, one by one, once you feel you've got control over the ones you've already worked on. *Do not try the impossible*. Sometimes you'll still be pushy, noisy, know-all, etcetera — and this

> is fine. It's part of you and there will be some of your friends and colleagues who love you for it. You just don't have to be these things all the time.
>
> 7   Set aside time each week to be on your own. Use it to think about the things done this week, the people you've talked to, the achievements in self-control you've made. This habit of introspection can be useful, once you've developed it, for the whole of your life.

Again, this strategy will not convert an Upfront Annie into a Shrinking Susie. But it should make an extrovert a little less overwhelming; and though most people would prefer to be over- rather than underwhelming it *is* something that needs control.

Not every aspect of personality can be covered here. There are so many subtle differences in all of us that it would be impossible. You will note, by the way, that nowhere have I referred to the so-called "Star Signs" — what effect it has on a person to be "born under Gemini" or "born under Cancer". That is because I believe it's all poppycock. How can people believe that the world is made up of just twelve kinds of people? And what about two people born in Australia and in the U.K. on the same day? The stars are in totally different positions — yet both have been born under whatever the date says the star sign is!

By all means read the starscopes in the paper to give yourself a giggle — but you're silly if you believe any of it.

QUESTIONS

Question 1   "I have a big bone structure and am embarrassed especially about my shoulders. People often comment on how broad they are. It makes me feel worse because all the girls of my age (16) are so petite. Could you please advise me as to how I can look more ladylike?"

You and Your Personality 65

Answer You don't have to do a thing to "look more lady-like". You are a girl — and that's all you need to be feminine. The world is full of handsome well-made 16-year-olds like you who are tall and broad and beautiful and sexy. Take a look at some of our super women athletes, some time! All you need do is look for pretty clothes that will make a feature of your splendid strong shapeliness, and walk tall with your head up and those shoulders back. And you'll look great!

Question 2 *"I am 13½ and I get so frustrated at my parents who won't let me join CND. They both fought in World War II and though they don't say it I am sure they feel that if there is another war it will be like the last and they will live through it. They say it will never happen, also that I'm too young to get involved with 'that CND' (their words). All they say is that I don't know what I'm talking about. I wish I could voice my opinion, but I have no idea who to contact."*

Answer Yes, it is difficult to deal with parents who don't realise that their babies have grown up into the intelligent young people that they are with political and social ideas of their own. Also, they could be afraid for your safety if you want to go on marches. And the more you nag them, the more stubborn they are likely to get. So don't nag. Instead talk to teachers at school to see if they can't start your own branch at school of the movement. Then, when your parents see that your views are shared by other responsible adults they trust, they may realise that the time has come to let you think your own political thoughts in your own way.

Question 3 *"I am 13 and think I'm going mad. My problem is I'm scared of going outside — and it's got worse as I've got older. I only have to walk down our road and I feel so conspicuous and self-conscious that I make a fool of myself. My parents are understanding about most things but they just say it's stupid shutting myself up in the house all day. They don't understand my problem and just joke about it. Should I see a head doctor, and how do I go about getting in touch with one?"*

Answer I am sorry your parents don't believe you, because in fact there are quite a number of school children of your age who develop phobias. This is the name given to a wide range of disabling fears with which people just can't cope. You seem to have agoraphobia, which means a fear of being in open places. You can get over this with the right help and your own family doctor can certainly arrange this. Or, you could ask one of the teachers at school — they'll be glad to put you in touch with expert help and make your parents see this is a real problem.

Question 4 *"I am 19 and have been going steady with my girlfriend for almost two years now. She really is very attractive and I think a lot of her but she has one great fault. Her language is filthy. I have tried talking to her about it but she just laughs at me or tells me not to be such a nancy boy. I wouldn't mind but she even uses four-letter words in front of my parents when she comes for tea. I plan to marry her soon but because of her language my parents are dead set against her. Is this normal and is there any way I can stop her swearing so much?"*

Answer You need to try to find out *why* your girlfriend swears so much. It could be that she regards it as a form of special intimacy. Some people get a big kick out of using "dirty" language with people they feel close to. Or, maybe she's trying to assert herself. There are girls who try to be liberated by using the sort of language they imagine is particularly masculine. Or, perhaps it's her way of being aggressive towards you, if she thinks you try to control her too much. Or it could be a bad habit — lots of people swear absent-mindedly. All you can do is talk to her about *why* she swears, but *don't complain*. That will just put her back up and make her swear more, I suspect. It's calm discussion that's the key here.

Question 5   "Am I a freak? Just because I don't go out as much as everyone wants me to, does that mean I'm abnormal? I'm not a very sociable person, more a home lover really. I'd rather curl up with a good book or watch TV, but that's not acceptable to my parents. If I tell them that I hate night life, my parents talk about me as if I had some sort of an illness. I'm crying as I'm writing this letter because I don't know what to do. If my parents are not proud of me, should I leave home? It's not as if I'm a lonely person. I have lots of friends and make friends easily. I get asked out by boys and whistled at by males of all ages. Please tell me I'm normal. I'm not a freak am I?"

Answer   No, of course you're not a freak — and your parents aren't cruel. They're a bit tactless, that's all. And that's no reason to leave home! Far from not being proud of you, they think you're lovely and long to see you having fun and enjoying all the joys and heady excitement of the courting days, and can't see how you're going to do all that sitting with them watching TV. All you need do is tell them firmly what you told me — that you have lots of friends, lots of fun and *lots of time*. If you prefer staying home nights now while you're 17 that doesn't mean you still will be when you're 27. It's my guess that once you reassure them that you're a happy friendly soul, they'll relax and leave you in peace. And then one day when you do start to go out and about they'll complain you're never home! But there, that's what being a parent is all about.

CHAPTER THREE
YOU AND YOUR PARENTS

QUESTIONS

Question 1   "I am $17\frac{1}{2}$ and feel at this age I should be out enjoying myself. The problem is my dad. He's constantly telling me what to do. I used to go out every night, but since I've been going out with my boyfriend my dad refuses to let me out more than once a week. He won't let me go down to our village to where everyone congregates. He says it makes me look cheap. He even chooses my friends for me. Both my friends had the same problem as me but now they are free to do what they like because they ran away from home and took an overdose. If things continue as they are with my dad I will do the same thing as I am so depressed."

Answer   Threatening to make silly gestures like running away and/or pretending to take an overdose is no way to convince your dad that you are mature enough to run your own life, is it? I do agree he is being a bit over-protective in trying to stop you from sharing the ordinary social life of the young people of your village, and from having a boyfriend to be with two or three times a week, but trying your friends' blackmailing techniques is certainly not going to make him behave in a more reasonable manner. First, you need an ally to help you persuade him to let you grow up — and it's the loss of your childhood, of course, that is upsetting him so much! — and the obvious person has to be your mum. Talk to her, and see if she can't help him let go a little. Or maybe an aunt, or a grandma can intervene on your behalf. And, why not ask him if you can invite the friends you meet, as well as your boyfriend, home one evening? When he meets them for himself and sees they're perfectly ordinary and respectable young people he might be reassured.

Question 2 "We have been a very close knit family — a daughter of 17 and a son of 15. My problem is my relationship with my daughter. She is very intelligent — has eleven 'O' levels, is studying three 'A' levels. I have tended to be the sort of mother who does everything for the family — they have a 'taxi service' by me to and from school and anywhere else they are going. My daughter has been studying for the past two years and so has not been asked to do any chores etc. around the home. I feel she has had things too easy and is now consequently lazy. The thing that has upset me most over the past six months or more is that she has shut herself away in her room only seeming to come down with the rest of the family for meals. I feel she is using the home and me for her convenience and cannot be bothered to socialise with us. She says as soon as she goes to university at 18 she will want to leave home. I am very hurt by her attitude and feel I have done all I can to establish a good home and close relationship which is now being thrown in my face. Was it worth all the sacrifice and caring when she doesn't seem to care about us any more? My husband feels that I am taking things too much to heart and that all teenagers are like this though my son is not at all like his sister and is very much family minded."

Answer You should be glad rather than sorry. You have done what all parents surely want to do — reared a child to fulfil all her potential, and be an independent successful adult. Her need to spend time alone, apart from you, isn't a reflection on you. It simply means she has found herself and has less need of you than once she had. That's something to be pleased about. Your resentment of her "laziness" is really based on your own realisation that she doesn't need that sort of childlike care any more. As for feeling that she is throwing your home and love in your face because she wants to leave it — well, every child has to leave eventually. In a couple of years probably, your family-minded son will be just as eager to go — because clearly you'll be as successful with him as you've been with her. It takes time to find the new equal-adult relationship that parents have with grown-up children, but if you relax, you'll find it will come. And it will be better than the mummy-little girl one you used to have.

Question 3 *"I am at my wits' end because my eldest son, 15½ years, and my husband can't stand the sight of each other. My son was a bit spoilt when younger, I know. He has quite a bit of freedom, but at school he is lazy, tiresome and regularly falls out with some teachers. He has also been caught smoking, and buying alcohol under age. These, I know, are hazards of reaching that "funny age". I understand this and have talked reasonably to him, but he can be so rude to me when I try and give advice. He is also very cruel to his little brother lately. He seems to enjoy hurting him. Now my husband has no patience, and the lad is retaliating. It's got to the stage where I have to get bodily between them to stop my husband hitting him. Both say the other is selfish, unreasonable and has no respect. My marriage is very happy, but I feel now there is a strain. My husband, by the way, was also spoilt and had everything his own way."*

Answer There are two different strands to your problem. One is that you have spoiled your son in the past, *and you still are*. Yes, some teenagers do become noisy and difficult as they hit their growing years, but that doesn't mean they have to be allowed to behave rudely and selfishly. I'm all for being an understanding mum — dead against being a doormat one. If the boy is rude to you, cruel to his brother, ill-mannered at school, and law-breaking, then his dad has every reason to be angry with him and say so firmly. Which brings in the second strand. I dare say your husband might have been a spoiled and difficult boy himself, and that contributes now to his reaction to his son. But there can be friction like this between the most placid of men and the best behaved of almost-adult boys based on natural masculine rivalry. That can sort itself out with goodwill and patience, as the boy grows older and the father learns to relax — but in your family you're making matters worse by so obviously taking sides. That allows your lad to exploit the situation. He knows exactly how to get both of you upset. Stop over-protecting him and let his dad sort out his dealings with him. If you refuse to join in the fights that will work better than what you're presently doing. Which is, frankly, stirring up trouble. Leave them alone to get on with it. It's their relationship. Only they can make it work.

Question 4 *"Our 15-year-old daughter was caught shoplifting. Thankfully she only got cautioned but the affair still makes me cry and feel ill. I hate to say this but my feelings towards her have changed. I've lost all interest in her. We were so close, but not any more. I feel as if I'm carrying a brick wall on my head. I have a very good husband. He was hurt very much too but he is more forgiving. I'm the sort of person who can't forgive."*

Answer You're not going to like what I'm going to say, but I'm going to say it all the same. Your hardness towards your daughter is based not on concern for her, but on your own conceit. You can't bear to face the fact that anyone connected with you is less than perfect. You want to believe that everything about you and yours is way above the ruck of common humanity. Common humanity makes people slip sometimes, makes them do things they shouldn't. But you can't forgive that in *your* child.

Hence your unrelenting attitude. Please, be honest with yourself. Look deep inside yourself and far back into your past. Did you never do sinful things? And did not the people around you forgive you for them? If you've really been so perfect all your life, then fair enough, go on as you are, demanding the same from others. But if you've ever slipped — and you *must* have done — surely you can find it in you to be *really* good, and to forgive and forget.

For a lot of young people parents are Acts of Nature, like mountains or lakes or the stars in the sky; they just *are*. You don't question the whys and wherefores of mountains and lakes much, so why question parents? Yet they are, of course, individuals with individual needs and reactions and worthy of attention. And, anyway, on a purely selfish level, you can't really understand yourself properly until you have some understanding of your parents. The people who have looked after you since you were born and who are still responsible for you are obviously people who have a lot to do with how you feel and how you think and how you behave.

And please note that the people who have done and are doing this for you may not necessarily be your natural, that is biological parents. Most young people may live with their biological parents — but lots don't. There are adopting parents and foster parents and step-parents and temporary parents, all sorts of parents. And they're all parents. Merely having sex and getting pregnant and giving birth to a baby doesn't make a person a true parent. It's the day in day out looking-after-and-living-with that matters.

So, if you happen to be adopted or fostered or to have one or more step-parents, try not to talk about the people who gave you birth as your "real" parents. They may have been your *first* parents, but they're no more real than the ones who are giving you care now.

So, whoever they are, how do you understand them?

You may have parents who have already told you a lot about what you weren't around to see for yourself. The way they met, for example, and how they got engaged and married, if they did. The reasons they split if they did, and remarried if they did. If so, you may think you actually know all you need to know about them, but you may be surprised to find out you've got it wrong.

So, a strategy to know your parents.

This is a strategy you may not even be able to begin. It all depends upon the sort of people your parents are. Some are very approachable on personal matters. They tend to be the sort of people who regard themselves and their children as pretty well equals, even though they themselves obviously have control over the family because they are older and have financial power.

There are other parents, however, who are just as loving and just as concerned about their children, but who feel that the right way to express that love and concern is to be very much "above" their children. It's not that they try to put their children down precisely; it's more that they see their role as being superior. In time they are likely to relax this attitude but not until their children are very much adults: usually when they are married and have children of their own. Then they may talk about their relationships with each other, their own young experience, their own needs and disappointments or fulfilments. *But any attempt to rush this sort of confidence can be very distressing to them.* They are not unloving or uncaring if they are not approachable on a purely personal level by their teenage children; they are just the way they are, and they have the right to be respected for being the way they are.

So, think hard. *Are* your parents likely to be offended if you start asking them personal questions? If you feel they might be then leave them alone. Don't label them as unloving, or uninterested. Just accept that this is how they are.

If you're sure they're the sort who will enjoy sharing themselves with you, then the chances are you'll romp through this strategy without any trouble. It's likely you already know a great deal about them and their past and their attitudes anyway; they'll have told you without any prompting!

If you're in any doubt then try step one, and read step two *carefully*.

STRATEGY
to know your parents

1   Tell them first that you've decided to get to know them better. Tell them it's not because you're just nosy, but because you're interested, because you want to feel even more

comfortable with them than you do (or to become comfortable if you don't!) and ask them to join in.

2   If they prefer not to *then don't nag about it*. If your parents are determined not to co-operate with this voyage of discovery *go no further*. This strategy is not for you.

3   If your parents are happy about co-operating, write a short account of your view of their life stories. Ask them — one, or better still both! — to tell you the true story. Then, compare the stories. Talk about the facts you got wrong — which you probably will! — and see if you can work out where you get your mixed-up ideas from. (This stage can be great fun as well as very illuminating. Hearing how your mum and dad got their love lives organised, for example, will help you see them in a very different light!)

4   Ask each parent in turn to tell you the things they like about the way they live now, covering home, job, friends, activities in general.

5   Ask them each to tell you the things they *don't* like about how they live now — and what, when they were your age, they wanted their lives to be like when they grew up.

6   Compare what they say. Are they more contented than discontented? Are they pleased with their achievements or disappointed? Have they got out of adult life what they wanted?

7   Ask them to make a list of the things about themselves they dislike. Then ask them to list

the things they *do* like (for example in the dislike list might be "fat", "impatient", "disorganised", "bad tempered in the mornings"; while on the likes list might be "sporty", "cheerful", "sympathetic", "kind" — and so on).

8   Make your list of what *you* think they'll put on their lists. Not what you personally like or dislike about them, but what you think *they* feel about themselves.

9   Compare the lists. How surprised are you? Do you actually know them as well as you thought you did?

10 Now go back to step *four* and do each stage *for yourself*. In other words, list your own likes, dislikes and so on, and ask your parents to join in and see if they understand your feelings and needs, and to comment on your lists as you did on theirs.

11 How much better do you feel you know each other now? Do you feel sympathy for the things in life that have disappointed your parents? Do you feel anger on their behalf for the bad things other people did to them? Do you feel proud of them for achieving what they have? Do you admire them for their sensible ways? Or do you feel they wasted their opportunities in a way that you won't? That they should have done things differently, worked harder or behaved differently?

Mixed up feelings are normal — you'll probably have lots of them. Just as they do now and will in the future about *you*.

WARNING. If at any point in this strategy you find you're arguing more than you're talking and discovering, STOP. This strategy is meant to help you understand each other, not to make you fight. Mind you, it's not necessarily a bad thing to fight with people you love — it's normal and natural, in fact. You'd have to be a vegetable not to have rows sometimes. But they ought to be constructive fights — teaching you things about yourself and each other. If this strategy causes rows that are destructive, then abandon it. It works marvellously for some people, but not for others — it's no failure in you or your parents if you're not the sort it works for!

There are other aspects of your parents' experience that you could discover — and one interesting one is why they're your parents at all.

Why do they have you? Were you a planned baby, or one who just happened?

Were they excited when they found out they were pregnant (and never forget it takes two to be pregnant — it's not just a woman's business) or frightened silly (and babies can terrify young inexperienced people)?

What changes did you cause in their lives? Did your mother have a job she had to give up? Did your father have to abandon career plans in favour of making more money because he was to be your father?

All these questions are well worth asking, once again with the warning that it's not clever to nag if they prefer not to answer.

The generation gap

People talk a lot about the wide chasm that is supposed to yawn between young people and their parents, putting a lot of emphasis on the effects of the age difference. You sometimes get the impression that people differ not because of their personalities but only because of their ages — that everyone who is ten likes the same sort of things and thinks the same sort of way, that everybody who is seventeen matches in the same way, and that all older people think in tune.

But if you look around you with your eyes properly open it will be obvious this isn't true. All the people in a class of ten-year-olds don't like all the same things — some enjoy music and some prefer sport and some love reading and some arithmetic. You know, of course, that the same is true of your own age group — some people you know are potty about pop, others are suckers for sport, some couldn't care less about either. It's what you *are* that matters, and will all your life, not what age you are.

So, the age difference between you and your parents doesn't matter as much as the differences in the way you think and feel.

However, what might matter is not the actual age gap between you, but the age at which your parents gave you birth. In some cases, a girl who has had a baby when she is, say, eighteen, makes a great job of rearing her child and they get on well.

In others, however, a teenage mother feels tied and resentful of her baby, because he or she prevented her from living her own life the way she might have preferred. So, the attitude gap between her and her child, when the child reaches teens, can be great.

Similarly, someone who waits to have her babies when she is in her middle to late thirties may be a better mother because she's older, more experienced in loving, having had time to live for herself for a while; or may be tense and anxious and set in her ways because she wasn't able to adapt to motherhood after so many years of living her own life. As I've said already, many times, *people vary*.

Hopes and fears

One of the most difficult things to do when you're young is to see yourself in relation to your parents. You can see them in relation to *you* without any difficulty: the way they behave to you, the things they say to you, the methods they use in caring for you affect you a lot and you know a great deal about them. But what about the way *they* feel about you?

There's *love*, probably. (Not undoubtedly. We have to be honest here and call the shots the way they fall; and the truth is that not all parents are able to give that selfless undemanding love that children so much want. It's not the end of the world if parents don't love their children; it's a pity, of course, both for child and the parents — but it need not destroy the child for ever! Young people can get their love from lots of other sources.)

There's possibly a strong sense *of duty*: "I gave you birth, so I owe you care —" If the duty is taken up uncomplainingly, then it's part of love; if it is taken up resentfully, then it's part of problems.

And there's *investment*. People put a lot of themselves into babies. They invest in their own physical future, in a way: when you have a baby, you're passing on bits of your own body to tomorrow. Whatever you may believe about life after death and Heaven and Hell, their existence is unproven, but a real live child is evidence that you will go on living. Which is one of the reasons parents feel so intensely about their children — and why they want to have grandchildren.

On a more mundane level, there are other sorts of investment, too.

Time — all those long nights sitting up with a bawling baby, all those long days spent playing with and feeding and nappy changing and the rest of it. And there's money — and that which creates money, a person's labour, either of body or mind. To have brought you to the stage you're at someone somewhere has worked very hard indeed to get for you the food and clothes and shelter you use.

Add all that together, and it's clear that parents give a lot to their children, and even the most selfless of them need some sort of reward. At the bottom level, maybe what they hope for is being financially secure and taken care of in their old age. For some it's not money but the desire to be loved and respected in their old age. For virtually all, it's the hope that the children they have will live happy successful lives. Seeing someone you care about being busy and successful and content can make you bust your buttons with pleasure and self satisfaction.

All of which most young people will find perfectly reasonable — as long as they and their parents have the same views on what makes a successful and contented adult. If you think it's being a footloose property-free rover with a knapsack on your back, traipsing the world and enjoying it, and they think it's being a bank official with a nice house and garden and three tidy children then you aren't going to see eye to eye at all.

So, the last strand in your understanding of parents — and yourself in relation to them — is to get them to make their *HOPE CHART* for *your* life. Copy out the chart opposite and ask them to fill it in under each heading. Then do the same yourself on a separate sheet of paper.

To use this chart, rate the importance of the various strands on a scale of one to ten. *Remember that some are mutually exclusive.* For example, job satisfaction involves pleasure in work apart from money, whereas early financial success may mean doing a job that bores you. So, you can't rate both those highly. If you think that money matters exactly as much as job satisfaction, then you'll give each of them a score of five. Similarly family closeness and freedom to travel cancel each other out.

Now, fill in the squares *below* your score — thus if you give nine to academic success fill in the tenth square only. If you give nil, fill in all the squares. If you give it 10 fill in no squares.

The resulting pattern of blank squares is your hope chart. If you have used tracing paper, you can now set your parents' chart on top of yours to see where you match, and where you don't. Otherwise look at them side by side.

You may be in accord about what matters in your future life, in which case, no hassle. But if you have very different patterns you have a lot to talk about. Like *why* you feel as you do — both of you!

HOPE CHART

	Academic success followed by professional career	Big earnings at an early age	Job status (apart from money)	Busy social life	Early marriage and children	Freedom to travel	Freedom from respon- sibility	Long term security	Public attention — and fame if possible	Continuing family closeness
1										
2										
3										
4										
5										
6										
7										
8										
9										
10										

All through your search for understanding of your parents, and the way you relate to them, be aware of the fact that you're walking on eggshells. If it hurts to find out facts about yourself that you don't much like — and so far in this book you will have probably found out several such facts — it hurts even more sometimes to find out things about people you care about. But good living doesn't mean hurtless living. People who never get hurt never get satisfaction, either. So, if after going through your strategies and checks with your parents you find their clay feet are more soggy than you thought they were, don't despair. Because unless you really are a very selfish and unloving person indeed, you'll find you'll still love them, and in fact love them rather more because you see them more clearly.

It takes real care and concern to set out on understanding people. But I can assure you that nothing you've found out can or will damage your relationship with your parents long term. It can only strengthen it.

CHAPTER FOUR

YOU AND YOUR OTHER RELATIVES

The more ingredients you have in a mixture, the more delectable the cake is likely to be — and the more things there are that can go wrong in the making. Families are the same. The more people there are in the group, the more cross currents and eddies are set up. (Note: That is a mixed metaphor. I like mixed metaphors, but some people hate them so much they go blue if they hear or read one. Fortunately there is no one in my family who feels that strongly, but if there were, my addiction to mixed metaphors would be part of the eddying cross currents caused by our cake making —)

If you have several ingredients to deal with — that is, you have brothers and/or sisters, there is information in this chapter that should be of use to you. *Even if you have not, read on*. Because all children meet and become involved with people with brothers and sisters and are therefore affected by this important relationship.

To make reading easier for everyone (and writing easier for me) I propose to stop using the clear but rather long brothers-and-sisters and instead will use the term siblings (or sibs, for short). This is quick and easy shorthand even if it is a bit jargonish.

The way you feel about your sibs depends heavily on where you come in a family.

If you're the *oldest* then the next child to come along to bless your parents' union comes to blight your life. Where once you reigned supreme as Baby-in-residence now you have to step aside to become Ex-Baby. As you all grow older, and others come to join the shuffling throng, you are made to feel more and more the responsibility of your senior position in the family.

If you're the *baby* of the family, then you're a loser before you begin. However hard you try, you can never be as clever, as big, as toothy, as *everything* as the others are. You're alternately over-protected or bullied or indulged or cheated and generally put upon by the rest of the family.

And if you're a *middle* you get clobbered in all directions at once. You've no chance of ever catching up with that superior Oldest, no hope of getting the extra coddling consideration that is lavished on the Baby.

Or, you may — if you are unusually fortunate — feel that your situation, be it oldest, middle or youngest, is ideal. In which case bully for you — but believe me, for the majority life as a sib has several drawbacks.

And of course, parents behave differently to each child, depending on where they come in the family. They may love them equally, but experience tempers everything, and the anxious careful first-time mother can be a cheerful casual leave-'em-alone one by the time she's had her third or fourth. And some parents get tired and dispirited; if you're well off and have a loving spouse, caring for a series of children can be enjoyable and not too arduous; but if you're a parent alone, and security is conspicuous by its absence, then that series of children becomes a burden, not a joy.

Add into the cake mix such matters as different personalities and different genders, and it will be clear that coping with sibs can be a difficult problem for young people.

It can be quite difficult for parents too.

Only children — winners or losers?

Does this mean that being an only child is the best thing to be? It's got a good deal going for it, obviously. You get all the parental loving and concern and involvement and loot that's going.

(And don't let anyone ever tell you money and possessions don't matter. They matter like the very devil, as anyone who has ever experienced real need knows. To want food and clothes is painful. To want a three-speed bike and the latest records and cassette players is painful too; if to a different degree. Most people, however high-minded and however oblivious of wealth, care a certain amount about possessions.)

The drawbacks to being an "only" are often talked about. "It's lonely," some say. "It makes you selfish," say others. "Only children are shy" and "Only children are pushy", and so on and so on.

Try this strategy for deciding which it is most comfortable to be, an only or one-of-a-brood. Use it whatever your own situation is; it will not only help you cope with your own feelings; it will help you understand the reactions of any friends you have who are in a different situation from you.

STRATEGY
for one or many

1. Make a list of all the good things you can think of about being an only child.

2. Make a list of the good things you can think of about being one of many.

3. Now, match each item on your list with its opposite. (For example, if you listed for Onlies, "No one to interfere with your things", then the opposite may be "Loneliness". And if you list as a pro on the One-of-Many's list "Plenty of companionship", then match it with the obvious "Lack of privacy".

4. Wherever you have a matched pair of pros and cons, cancel them out. The good balances the bad, so you have no problems, whatever your situation (Only or One-of-Many). Now look at what is left.

5. If what you have left is a pro for someone in your situation, then be happy; you like the way you are. There is no need to go further.

6. If you are left with cons about your situation, then consider into which category they fall:
   a) Things that cannot be changed by anyone.
   b) Things that can be changed by others' effort.
   c) Things that can be changed by your own efforts.

   I can't tell you how to make the selection; only you know the factors you're dealing with, and only you can identify which are changeable, which not. *Think hard.*

7   Those that are in category (a) must be endured. They're like the colour of your eyes or the shape of your nose — an inevitable part of you and your life. So, *forget them*. Get on with living.

8   Those in category (b) that can be changed by others need the help of those others. Are they willing to offer the help? If you can show that you've thought carefully about the situation you want changed, will they co-operate in any ideas you have for action on their part which will help you?

   Example: You are an only child. You are lonely. And after you've sorted out all the other pros and cons of your situation you realise that your loneliness is due not only to being an only child; it's also because you and your parent(s) live in a remote village far from school. Once you get home each day you can't meet school friends again, because of the distance problem. So you have no social life as well as no sibs to share with. The only remedy for the long lonely evenings and weekends is either for the whole family to move home nearer school, or, if this is impracticable, for your parents to agree to make other plans for you, perhaps arranging for you to lodge near school with a friend's family, coming home for occasional weekends and holidays from time to time. *Be aware of the fact that the cure might be as bad as or worse than the problem.* Using the example above, the homesickness you might suffer from being a boarder-out might be worse than the loneliness you suffer being at home all the time.

9   You are now left with category (c), those con factors which *you* can change.

Do you really want to change them?

Sometimes people complain about aspects of their lives because it is useful to have something to complain about, something you can blame for your difficulties or failures. Take away the problems and you may be left with more disagreeable ones.

Example: You feel that as an only child you experience too much supervision and control from your parents, and you'd like to leave their home and be free. Ask yourself then if you want to do without the care and coddling that usually comes packaged with this sort of over-protection, and also ask yourself honestly whether you actually need the control they exercise: could you be sure you could control your own life safely if you left home altogether?

If you get the answers you need to this self-questioning, the next step is

10 MAKE THE CHANGES. (Difficult? Absolutely. No one promised anything would ever be easy.)

People with sibs tend, in my experience (here I speak both as one who has three sibs and also is the parent of three children) to have problems which fall into two major groups.

First, the togetherness of family life which is forced on you.

Second, the jockeying for privilege, position and attention; and resentment due to failing to win what you want.

Examples: A girl might complain that because she has sisters and she has to share a bedroom with them, they meddle with her belongings. That's a group one problem.

A boy might complain that when he was fifteen or so he was controlled regarding bedtimes, friends and activities much more than his younger brother is being controlled, now he has reached fifteen. That is a group two problem.

Look at them closely, these groups, and you'll see that in fact they are precise opposites. People with group one problems are complaining because they are not able to live as individuals. They want to be just themselves, not lumped together with sibs and forced to share everything with them.

People with group two problems, on the other hand, are complaining because they *do* want all the sibs to be lumped together, and do not want individual members of the family to have individual experiences or benefits.

Since at some time or another most people with sibs will make complaints about problems in both groups, it will be seen that by and large people are not logical about this complex relationship.

In fact, what many people who complain about their sibs are saying to their parents is, "Treat me as an individual, but treat them as a lump."

No wonder that some parents feel despairingly that a parent's place is in the wrong!

Living with sibs

Some of the problems you have had with your sibs over the years you will have learned to solve yourselves. You may, in order to stop a sib from, for example, borrowing your gear without asking, have used *democratic* methods, free and open discussion, an offer to lend as long as you're properly asked, and an arrangement to borrow his/her gear on request.

Or you may have opted for

financial methods (paying him/her regular bribes in cash or kind to keep hands off your property), or
preventive methods (covering everything with combination locks), or
despotic methods (beating the hell out of him/her whenever your gear is touched without your permission), or
retaliatory methods (taking his/her stuff and ruining it), or
consultation methods (getting your parents involved), or
others of your own devising.

All or any of these work, depending on the person with whom you are dealing. Some sibs are perfectly amenable to the democratic approach, sharing your sense of natural justice and good behaviour, and acquiescing gracefully in your scheme for ensuring peace in the home. Other sibs are too thick/too insensitive/too selfish/too spoiled (you'll know which it is) to respond to any but tough methods. If you have found that your technique works reasonably, keeping your gear safe while avoiding too many uproars round the house, fair enough. Stick to that method.

But if you find that you've not yet managed to find a way to resolve the difficulty, it may help you to use a flowchart technique for deciding how to handle a problem. The flowchart will work for any kind of problem that occurs between you.

Like or not like

Some of the more tiresome problems that arise between sibs are due to the fact that, though you share the same parents (or perhaps one parent, because of course sibs can be step-brothers and sisters) and live in the same home, you may well be wildly different in tastes, abilities and aptitudes. Unfortunately, there are lots of adults, who should certainly know better, who assume that the fact that you are sibs means you are alike, and that any disparity between you is due to your own bloody-mindedness, not a natural difference.

It's bad enough when outsiders get this notion that sibs Ought To Be Alike and therefore Ought To Love Each Other — it's even worse when you are infected with the idea yourself. You feel very guilty and somehow less than human when you discover that deep inside yourself you absolutely loathe one or other of your sibs. You blame yourself for being a failed person, rather than the irrational idea that merely being born of the same family ties you into bonds of love. It ties you into

YOU HAVE A PROBLEM WITH A SIB

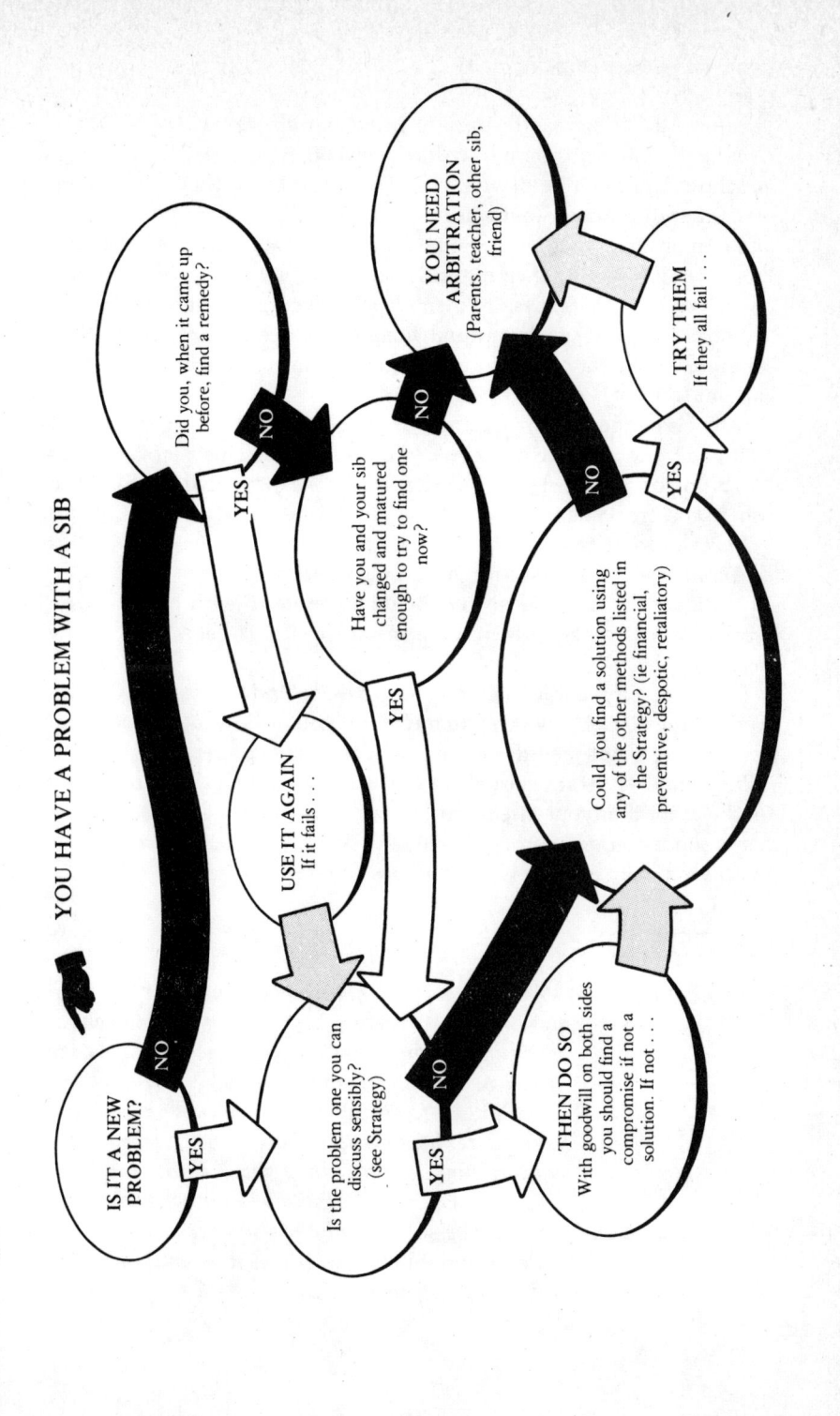

IS IT A NEW PROBLEM?

— NO → Did you, when it came up before, find a remedy?
  - YES → **USE IT AGAIN** If it fails...
  - NO → Have you and your sib changed and matured enough to try to find one now?
    - YES → (continues to discuss sensibly)
    - NO → **YOU NEED ARBITRATION** (Parents, teacher, other sib, friend)

— YES → Is the problem one you can discuss sensibly? (see Strategy)
  - YES → With goodwill on both sides you should find a compromise if not a solution. If not... **THEN DO SO**
  - NO → Could you find a solution using any of the other methods listed in the Strategy? (ie financial, preventive, despotic, retaliatory)
    - YES → **TRY THEM** If they all fail...
    - NO → **YOU NEED ARBITRATION** (Parents, teacher, other sib, friend)

bonds of relationship and habit, of course — but not necessarily more than that.

Unloving feelings can be born of so many different things, that's the trouble. People who might have liked each other very well if they'd met as schoolmates can be driven apart by the fact that they suffer from severe family jealousy that was badly managed when they were babies, and remains to plague them. Some parents are very effective at helping their young cope with their natural feelings of resentment and suspicion of each other; others, despite their efforts never quite get it right — so the children grow up in mutual hostility. Once they're adults they separate with great relief and exchange Christmas cards but do all they can not to meet.

If this is happening to you and your sibs then it's happening. *Accept it*. If you try too hard to overcome your dislike you'll just increase it. It's like biting on a painful tooth. Better to face the fact you don't like each other, and create as much space around you as you can.

Plan not to be together more than you must.

Avoid direct confrontation if you possibly can.

Cultivate the habit of always being as polite to each other as you would be to strangers. It may be insincere, but it helps to keep the peace.

Do it that way, and you may be surprised to find that as time goes on some of the dislike between you melts and you mellow into respect and acceptance, if not the full blown love you'd have preferred.

Incidentally, most people find that however much they personally loathe a sib, if anyone else starts to make nasty comments about him/her, a sudden surge of protective loyalty comes up. *You* can hate 'em — but heaven help anyone else who does. Interesting, isn't it?

QUESTIONS

Question 1 "When I was 15 my mum and dad never let me go to gigs or late parties and kept on at me about school work and so on. Now my younger brother is the same age — he's three years younger than I am — he's allowed to do all sorts of things that would have made them go up the wall when I was 15. If I say anything about it they say it's not true, that they treat us the same, though I know they don't. It wouldn't be so bad only he's so cheeky to me. If I say anything to him he ignores it, even though I'm telling him for his own good."

Answer There are two different things happening here. One is that your parents have learned in their dealings with you how to be more relaxed and comfortable with your brother. I'm sure they believe they're treating both of you the same, and indeed mean to, but memory plays tricks, even over a mere three years, and their experience has modified their parenting practices. Though in fact it's unlikely that they are really all that much more lenient with your brother, they will seem to be so because the fact you've grown up so successfully has made them less anxious. And what you remember as much as any real control is the tension that was in them at the time. But all that, maddening though it is for you with your memories of how frustrated you used to feel, isn't quite as maddening as the fact that your brother is growing up and no longer regards you as quite the God he once did. I've no doubt that in his younger years he was much more in your shadow. That he looked up to you, copied you, listened to what you said because that is, by and large, what happens with younger brothers (even if they hide their admiration under cheekiness). But he's growing up now, and that means he's growing out of his dependence on you just as much as he's growing out of his need for Mum and Dad. And that can hurt the person being grown out of a good deal. All you can do is be patient. In another two or three years, you'll find that the gap between you has narrowed and you'll feel far more like equals and be less in need of establishing your own adult status in his eyes. And then you should be free of these lingering childhood jealousies and be able to enjoy him as a friend rather than just as a kid brother.

Question 2 *"When my sister was 16 she got pregnant and had to get married. It caused terrible rows in the family. Now, she's all settled and gets on great with Mum and Dad — she's 22 now and has two children — and sides with them when they won't let me do things like go out to discos and have boyfriends. It's all her fault they treat me so hard, and yet she never* backs me up. It's not fair because I'm not a bit like her. She was always in a rush to get her own way; I always stop and think, truly I do. I'm 15 by the way. We have awful rows all the time over it but they just tell me I'm childish."

Answer   Well, you could be right and your parents could be being more controlling with you because of your sister's experience. Or it could be that they are treating you just as they treated her while hoping that you won't make the same mistakes she did. After all, you were only eight when the problem happened, so your memory is likely to be hazy about it all, isn't it? But *they* remember — because too young illegitimate pregnancies cause great distress in families, and though it's all turned out well for your sister now, they're very aware of how unhappy they were at the time. And naturally, they want to avoid the same misery affecting you. I know you feel it's unfair that they should be treating you simply as your sister's look-alike rather than as a person in your own right, but if you can be more tolerant of their behaviour, and recognise it for what it is — concern for you rather than control for its own sake — it will help you to talk to them sensibly about your needs instead of having rows with them. If you shout and get angry when you can't do what you want to do, that will convince all three of them that you're still a baby, because that's babyish behaviour. But if you can be reasonable and explain you understand their anxiety, but feel they are not going the right way about helping you learn how to avoid problems *for yourself*, you've got a better chance of having a social life of your own.

Question 3   "I'm 17 and an apprentice in a garage. I've got good prospects and my boss says I'll be a really good motor engineer. But my brother who is a year older is one of those bookish types and he's at college studying to be an accountant. And to listen to my parents going on and on you'd think he was the greatest egghead in the world. It's all 'my son at college' this, and 'my son at college' that. It's never 'my son in the garage'. You'd think they'd be pleased I'm doing well too, but I never hear them boasting about me. They're really snobs."

Answer Have you told them how you feel about the things they say to people in your hearing? It could be that they're the sort of parents who think it's somehow bad for a person to hear praise of themselves, and so never talk about you when you're within earshot — but stick to boasting about their absent son. And have you asked your brother what they say about you when you're not around? It could be he feels as jealous of their pride in your gifts as you do of him! It's a lot more talking that's the answer to this problem, you know. Because if in fact I'm wrong and they *do* show off more about him than about you, telling them how hurtful they're being could make them stop and think a good deal.

CHAPTER FIVE

YOU AND OTHER PEOPLE

Life can be complicated enough, dealing just with parents and sibs. Add on all the other relatives like grandparents and aunts and uncles — your parents' parents and sibs, so therefore important *in their* lives — and life gets even more complex.

Coping with other relatives

Take the matter of aunts, uncles and cousins, for a start. If you find yourself in rivalry with your sibs, and wanting to show them how much better you and yours are than they and theirs, you should understand why it is that your parents feel strongly — as many parents do — about the way you behave to these relatives. You are, in parental eyes, an extension of themselves. If you achieve something that ensures that they shine in the eyes of their own sibs they'll glow; if you make a cock-up, then they'll feel put down. Which is why it often happens that parents seem more agitated about the opinions of the family regarding your behaviour than they do about the way you feel.

And of course the same is true twice over when it comes to grandparents. When your grandparents react to you, your parents feel they are reacting to them as well — and if there has ever been any strife or tension in *that* parent-child relationship (and it's odds on there has been at some time) then you can bet your bottom dollar and sixpence more that you'll be the one in the line of fire if the grand-parental reaction is a disapproving one.

It cuts both ways of course; if you do something that makes your grandparents purr with approval of you, then your own parents will glow with twice the fire.

Cousins of course are involved in all this. Just as you will sometimes feel they are being paraded as objects of emulation for you, so will you be used against them by *their* parents, sometimes. If you can all understand why the elders are behaving like this, it might help you to build friendly relationships with your cousins; you'll see that it's not their fault they've been shown to you as Perfect Little Darlings — and vice versa. You'll become friends in spite of being related and certainly not because you are.

If you come from a family where everyone likes each other, across all the generations, and it's fun and giggles all the way when you're all together and not a hint of rivalry, fall on your knees in prayerful gratitude. You're in a minority of lucky people.

What about the neighbours?

As I said in the introduction to this book, the trouble with many adults is that they suffer from severe amnesia. You'd think they'd never gone through the complexities of growing up themselves when you listen to them mutter on and on about the way you're doing it.

Not all older ones behave like this, of course — there are plenty of people in their 50s, 60s and older who are civilised and civil, interesting, fun and a joy to know. But there are enough of the other sort to give all adults a bad name among the young — because they tend to be the noisiest. They're the sort who write letters to newspapers about how lazy and disgusting young people are nowadays etcetera.

Why? What is it about these older people that makes them so blindly anti-youth?

SOME may be *jealous*. It's hellish being 50 plus, with a dull life to live and missed opportunities in the past and a load of responsibilities you never really wanted in the present. These people hate the young because of their youth, looks and health. It's the only way they can live with themselves.

SOME may be *frightened* of you. From time immemorial, the young of every species have been a threat to the generation that produced them. You're all jostling for your precarious place in the sun, and each young new hopeful is a warning to the older ones that their time is passing, that soon they must step aside into the shadows. A nasty feeling — of course people who have it feel hate for their rivals. (Mark you, some of the punks around are enough to frighten anybody — especially very old and nervous people. It's worth remembering that although you may mean no harm, your appearance can scare the pants off someone.)

SOME may be *ignorant* of what it is you really mean. Each new fashion that comes along, be it in clothes, in music, in slang, is meant to be *new* — its whole purpose is to provide a fresh new identity for the people who follow it. The trouble is that some fashions of speech and behaviour may be the direct opposite of past fashions — and hard for other people to cope with.

For example, young people today use language that, a couple of generations ago, was regarded as literally unspeakable. Older people who were taught that certain words were violent and disgusting can't cope with the fact that now these same words are regarded as being harmless.

And, most important of all SOME may be *justified*. Just as not all adults are drearies and some are cheerful, open-minded and friendly, so not all young people are sensible, thoughtful and caring of others. Some are ill behaved yobs who trample all over others' feelings and needs and are downright cruel. They're the sort that give your generation a bad name. It's rough you get painted with their brush but — here we go again — life *is* rough.

The way you personally react to injustices dealt out by suspicious elders will have a profound effect on the people who are dishing them out. If you respond to their hostility with your own hostility you will be being natural; it's an almost inevitable response. But if you're clever, you won't be natural. You'll turn their hostility on *them* instead.

Coping with teachers

Teachers are people too.

That may sound like a somewhat patronising comment but it still needs to be made. They are, just as you are, very much affected by their personal experiences of life. When you go into a classroom to start a day's work, you don't abandon your involvement with and concern for your parents, your friends, your pleasures and your fears. They sit at your desk with you and tangle themselves in with your work.

If you're happy at home and elsewhere and you've got no problems, you'll work well and blossom.

If your parents are at daggers drawn with each other or you, if your friends are non-existent or miserable, if your life is full of problems, then the opposite happens.

The same happens to teachers.

The ratty person at the front of your class may have had a fight with his/her lover/spouse last night. There may be sick parents, indigestion, headache, a difficult landlord, a suicidal friend, a bad-tempered headmaster and sour colleagues in the common room all contributing to the scowl with which you, the pupils, are being regarded. But because young people are, by and large, unaware of such facts, they tend to assume that a teacher is being difficult or nasty just for the sake of it.

If you think about it, of course, it's obvious that teachers get more satisfaction from being cheerful than from being nasty. They must prefer to be liked by their pupils, to be able to spend forty minutes of shared interest each lesson rather than shared boredom, and generally doing their job happily.

So, if a teacher is a misery, *there is a reason*. And it will help you cope with your school life better if you understand that reason.

It's too easy for young people to get the feeling that *their* problems, *their* anxieties, *their* needs are paramount, and that all the adults with whom they deal ought to set aside their personal problems in order to concentrate on you — especially if they happen to be paid to do a job that involves you, like teaching.

Such thinking is childish.

Start showing teachers as well as parents and other older adults that you can give as well as take. And giving concern and understanding to a bad-tempered or less-than-perfect teacher is a good way to start.

All of which adds up to a very basic strategy indeed — and one that will sound extremely Victorian, but that is as fresh today as it ever was.

Do unto others as you would they would do unto you.

Politics in the classroom

It is not easy to develop an interest in politics if you see it as just interminable reports on TV and radio about party conferences, fights in the House of Commons, and older adults droning on and on about taxes and unemployment and the Unions and Everything Ought To Be Put A Stop To. It sounds, all of it, like something that has nothing whatsoever to do with real life, and certainly not to do with yours.

In fact, there's more to politics than party squabbles and complaining about the Government. Everything any of us ever does is, in its own way, a political statement, because politics is about living in groups.

You already know perfectly well the politics of being young. You suffer the injustices as well as the benefits of being in that particular pigeon-hole. But there are others you fit into, and you may be affected by them more than you realise.

The word "class" has come to be regarded as a dirty one. To talk cheerfully about some people being "middle class" and "upper class" and "working class" infuriates those people who look back to the days when society was heavily divided among these lines — when the haves (middle and upper classes) had it all and the havenots (working classes) had none. "Today," say these angry ones, "these divisions are irrelevant. Everyone should be equal."

Well, yes, everyone should — but saying that doesn't make it so. And the hard truth is that though society has changed, there are still class differences. Some people still have, and some still have not. Not just money and objects — but intelligence and attitudes and standards are included in the list of what people have and have not. Especially attitudes.

If you're a pupil, there is frankly not much you can do if people get at you on class grounds. There are even teachers who do it: they mimic pupils' accents or speech patterns, and generally make it clear to everyone that you're a complete outsider as far as they are concerned. And there are always crawlers in a classroom who like nothing better than to join in when a teacher picks on some pupils in that way, giggling and jeering in their turn, which adds to the misery.

Why do some teachers do it? *Often because of their own sense of inadequacy*. They feel insecure about their own origins and go into the attack, believing that that is the best method of defence.

There may be some comfort in being able to tell yourself that teachers who behave like this are insecure snobs, and deserve your scorn and pity rather than your distress. There is *no* comfort in the long term in going along with the opinion of such teachers and developing shame and disgust for your own origins and culture. Becoming like them is the last thing you want.

So, sit it out, grim though it is. Refusing to show any awareness of the digs and the criticism is in fact the best strategy; when tormented pupils blush, stammer and show they care, the tongues of such teachers and others are sharpened to a harder edge. Stonewalling is more likely to blunt them.

Colour Prejudice

This is much harder to deal with and anyone who says otherwise is a liar. Any person faced with criticism or unjust treatment on the basis of his colour would feel — rightly, I believe — deeply insulted at the suggestion that they deal with it by ignoring it, sitting it out or stonewalling. Stupid class prejudice deserves mere contempt; colour prejudice deserves vigorous response, for it is much more threatening — because it is much more obvious and permanent. You can change your speech and table manners if you care enough about such minor matters. But you can't change your colour — so you must live with it and be able to take joy in being as you are.

Anyone who is treated with obvious prejudice, who is jeered at or commented about on the basis of colour, should protest loudly; should complain about the person who has displayed this behaviour to his/her superiors; should use every effort they can to stop that person in his/her tracks.

But of course that's comparatively easy. Dealing with obvious colour prejudice is a matter of having courage, of standing up and demanding your rights. Other black people in other parts of the world are fighting this battle now as they have for years. They haven't won yet — but they're gaining ground, slowly, depending on the country they live in.

What is much more difficult is dealing with hidden prejudice, the sort of racial attitudes that are never actually put into words that you, as an individual, can seize on. When you're passed over for promotion in class or in a job though you know perfectly well that you're better than the person of a different colour who gets it. And when you complain you are told you are being over-sensitive.

How do you deal with that if it happens to you? First of all be prepared for the possibility that in some cases this may just possibly be true.

There are black people who are sloppy or lazy or ill-mannered or whatever who, whenever they miss out on anything because of these qualities, immediately shout "prejudice" instead of taking an honest look at themselves. They need to stop and think hard about what they're really doing because this reaction can actually create prejudice where none existed before. Something else that can have this effect is deliberate helplessness. Are you, if you're black and feel put upon, ever guilty of shrugging your shoulders and saying in effect, "It's a waste of time trying — everyone will be against me anyway because I'm black, so what the hell — I shan't bother?" If you do that, you could be making self-fulfilling prophecies.

Yes, there are prejudiced white people about who will mistreat you, pass you over, deprive you of your opportunities because of their prejudice. *But there are others who do not*. There are in all communities white people who do care for your welfare, white people who feel as sick as you do about the injustices some black people experience, white people who want to help. But they need your help in resisting these injustices. If you don't even try to fight for the education, the opportunities, and the justice you want and deserve, how can anyone else help you? Yes, it's a lousy world that makes it necessary for you to need help. It's a lousy world that contains bigots who illtreat you. But you won't make it any the less lousy by behaving foolishly — in fact you make it worse for yourself, easier for the bigots.

So, a working strategy for black people who have to face up to others' prejudice.

Watch out for ghettoism — hiding away from any aspect of non-black culture.

Watch out for the state of mind that makes you say, "All whites are bastards" just because some are. This is another form of nourishment for prejudice.

Watch out for the risk of defending the indefensible on grounds of colour alone — if a black mate breaks the law, protecting him just because he's black is being prejudiced yourself, once again. It's the fact that he's a law breaker that should weigh with you, not just the fellow feeling created by your shared skins.

Watch out for making devious use for your own ends of the existence of prejudice. For example, a boy I knew, one of a small group of black people at a big school, tormented smaller white boys, started fights, stole from them, generally stirred up trouble, and the moment a teacher arrived to sort out the resulting row announced loudly, "This boy insulted my race, sir!" Inevitably the teacher always took his side, terrified as many white people are of ever being accused of colour prejudice, and gave hell to the chaps the black boy had already given hell to. Not surprisingly he left a trail of black-hating schoolmates behind him all through the school.

There are a lot of don'ts in that strategy, aren't there? It sounds, all of it, just like the sort of soft liberal love-thy-neighbour attitudes that many deeply angry radical black people find almost as hateful as downright and obvious prejudice. You have every right to see it that way, and to choose different, more direct strategies. On the other hand, you could try it for a while, and see how it works.

Violence

You'd have to be blind, deaf and stupid not to have noticed a new dimension in schools in these nineteen-eighties. Violence. From time to time newspapers and TV bulletins erupt into hysterical accounts of schools being wrecked by rampaging students, of teachers being attacked, of heaven knows what sort of mayhem being committed by people who are still young enough to be regarded as children. Adults rush around asking each other in great agitation, "Why does it happen?" "How can we stop it?" "Who is to blame?" and getting no answers.

There are no simple answers — but certainly, in some cases, colour and religious prejudice (because everything I've said about class and colour applies to religious prejudice too) and the effects of living in a depressed high-unemployment area are likely causes.

Other times the reasons are more obscure.

These are massive social problems which need urgent and widespread remedies. But violence in schools (or in the streets), whatever the cause, will do far more harm than good. So if you hear rumbles of trouble brewing in your school or elsewhere; if you know that there are individuals spoiling for some violence:

Tell tales.

Too often it turns out after an outbreak of violence has been dealt with that a lot of the quieter more sensible people in the school (who are usually in the majority of course, but keep so quiet no one realises they are there in such numbers) knew what was in the air, but kept quiet because — well, because they were quiet types who don't want to get involved. But they *must*, because for evil to succeed it is necessary only that good men do nothing. If you let your school suffer an attack of violence because you minded your business, you're as bad as the people who actually kicked the windows in. There are times when it isn't sneaking to tell teachers, parents, any responsible adults, what you believe is happening. It's intelligent self-preservation as well as concern for others' welfare.

QUESTIONS

Question 1   "I am a lad of 18. Any time I go out I get very nervous and I feel like fighting anyone who says anything to me. I know this is not normal because people around me are quiet and calm and cool. Do you think any drug will calm my nerves down? I am worried because I can't control myself."

Answer   Well, at least you realise you've got a problem, which is more that some aggressive and violent young men do. And that means you can be helped. Talk to your doctor about your feelings, and ask him to arrange for you to see a psychotherapist, someone who is an expert in helping people sort out the tangle of feelings that so often lies behind violence. He may also suggest tranquillising drugs, although they are not the ultimate answer, since they can be a useful first step towards controlling your rage. If you feel unable to explain to your doctor, pick up the phone and ask the operator to put you through to the Samaritans. They're a great first line of help and can see to it that you get the further care you need.

Question 2   "*I am a girl of 13 and any time I'm watching a programme and the man and woman are kissing, my dad tells me to turn it off. I don't think it's fair. I'm a teenager now and they're only kissing. My dad gave me permission to watch the sex education programme at school, so I've seen it all, and more, so I can't understand why he won't let me see kissing at home.*"

Answer   It's not because he's worried about the effect of intimacy on the screen on *you*. It's because he gets all shy and uptight when he sees it that he makes you switch channels! He obviously had rotten sex education when he was a boy, and it's left him with all those uncomfortable feelings about seeing people being loving. Be glad he's done his best to see you get a better education by encouraging you to go to school classes, and don't fuss him about TV. It's not worth upsetting him, is it?

Question 3   "*I'm a girl aged 17. I've got a great boyfriend who will do anything for me, he's really considerate and loving. I used to think so highly of him when we first met. I was unemployed, he was in work and he helped me through each day with loving words of comfort and gave me confidence to get out and find work once again. Now I have a job but my boyfriend was made redundant. Since having no job, he's still the same loving person but I don't look up to him as I used to. He seems weak and unsure of himself which is natural, I know, but I can't seem to help him as he helped me. I know I have love for him in my heart and show it as much as I can, but I don't have as much as he has for me. How can I love him more, need him more, and care about him more? I've put myself in his place and tried to understand how he really feels but it doesn't seem to work.*"

You and Other People

Answer   I suspect that your problem is based on stereotyped ideas about what men and women should be like. You seem to feel, deep down, that it's all right for a girl to be vulnerable, frightened and in need of support, and that the most admirable men are those who can provide such girls with care and comfort. You do not seem willing to allow men to have the same sorts of needs as women or to have the same desire for reassurance. So, inside you're despising your boyfriend because he is as you were. Which is unkind to say the least! How do you cope with this sort of feeling? Well, with luck and good will you'll outgrow your rather narrow view of human nature and be able to give as well as get from your relationships. But meanwhile, you could try to help your boyfriend by drawing on another and different stereotype of what women are. Imagine that he is a young and vulnerable person *in need of mothering*. Then you may find it easier to give him the care he so badly needs at the moment. And as you'll find in the future all caring relationships involve a see-sawing of mutual support.

Question 4   *"I am a 15-year-old boy and there is this boy up my road who even though I have done nothing to him will not stop bullying me. I'm scared to go out because of him. I can't stand up to him because I've got nothing against him. Anyway, he'd bash my brains out. I hate fighting. Don't tell me to talk to my parents because they would only call me a coward which I don't think I am. Please give me a way out."*

Answer   It's a sad paradox that sometimes people who hate fighting and are pacifists at heart have to stand up and fight for the right to be peaceable. If this chap is bullying you then the only way he'll see sense is to be bullied back. Answering force with force is ugly, I know — in an ideal world people would always be amenable to sweet reason. But this is not an ideal world, which means that you sometimes need the threat of fists. If your own aren't enough in this case, and your parents are so unsympathetic, it has to be those of other people of your own age. It's my bet that if you recruited among people in your class at school you'd find a friend or two who'd like nothing better than a face-to-face argument with this bully, and would cheerfully come and help you sort him out. And once it's done, it's very likely he'll scoot off whenever he sees you in the future, for fear you'll bring your mates back. No need for any *real* fighting, you see. Just the fear of it can be enough to send a bully packing.

CHAPTER SIX
YOU AND YOUR FRIENDS

QUESTIONS

Question 1 "My daughter has taken up with a couple of girls I really can't stand. They swear a lot, they smoke, they're really uncouth, wear awful clothes, don't wash enough, everything you could think of. But she won't hear a word against them. I won't have them in the house of course, they're so awful. How can I help her see they'll lead her into bad ways? She's a very wilful 14 and I can't stand the rows we keep having."

Answer It takes two to have rows — and this one is largely of your making! To refuse to allow these girls to visit your home is to turn them into martyrs, to make them infinitely more glamorous and interesting and delightful to your daughter. Be sensible, do — *invite them home a lot*. The one of two things will happen. Either you will see what it is about them, beneath the exterior of which you so disapprove, that your daughter finds so entrancing, and learn to like them too (for after all she's your daughter and that means you've got a lot in common) or she, seeing them in the context of her own home will see what it is you dislike in them and grow away from them of her own free will. Certainly you've nothing to lose, everything to gain by dealing with the situation that way.

Question 2 "My trouble is that my parents are terribly prejudiced about my friends. All my friends are black *because I think black people are much nicer than white ones. I never want any other mates but them. They're more friendly and cheerful and their music is great and I have a marvellous time with them. But my mum and dad never stop going on and on about them because they're black and they make me really sick. I think it's prejudice that causes all the troubles in the world."*

Answer   You're absolutely right that prejudice causes a great many of the world's problems. Not all, mind you, but a lot. But can't you see that you are being just as prejudiced as your parents are? They display their bigotry against black people — but you're displaying yours against whites! If you said that you loved your friends just because of their cheerfulness and friendliness (as well as their music) that would be great. But you seem to think that they have these qualities *because* of their colour and not just incidentally. And that is prejudice. So think again. Do you choose your friends as a way of cocking a snook at your parents? Lots of people do deliberately choose mates who will upset their parents — it's a way of displaying their new independence of mind as they grow up. When you can say, hand on heart, that you choose your mates because they are people you like, and don't notice whether they are pink, purple or covered in sky blue spots, then and only then can you hurl accusations of colour prejudice at your parents. Until then, you're cut out of the same piece of cloth that they are.

Question 3   *"I am going out with a girl who is 15. I am 19 and her dad is going to stop her seeing me any more because he says I'm too old for her, but I don't think the ages matter as long as you are in love. She loves me very much so it will be upsetting for both of us if we have to split up. Her mum doesn't mind because she likes me but what can we do about her dad?"*

Answer Do try to see the situation from her dad's point of view. She *is* only 15 — little more than a child. Of course he is suspicious of a full-grown man — and at 19 that's what you look to him — coming along to threaten his care of her. Stop fighting him and start to co-operate with him and it's my guess you'll be able to keep your relationship going till she's old enough for him to relax a little more. Tell him you know how he feels and respect it, and ask his permission to visit her at his home, under his eye, on a regular basis. If your shared love is all you say it is, it will survive such chaperonage for a year or so — and by then her dad should see you less as a threat, more as a chap he can trust with his precious girl. This may be less fun for you both than being free to go where you like, when you like, but it's better than being forbidden to meet altogether.

Question 4 "My son is 16 and a quiet sort of boy but fully developed for his age. I worry about him because all his friends are so much younger than he is. He goes about with boys of just 14 or so, and no one of his own age though he knows I don't approve. My other son, when he was this age, had most of his friends a year or two older, which seems more natural to me and which I liked very much. I can't help thinking there's something unnatural about my younger son, but if I say anything he just shuts up like a clam."

Answer But why should it be all right for a boy of 16 to have friends of 18, but not to have friends of 14? You do seem to be in a hurry to make your sons grow up faster than they want to. The fact that your older son was willing to choose friends more mature than he was shows only that he was a resilient chap who could cope with the extra demands such friendships made on him. The fact that your younger son is resisting and seeking his companionship among less demanding younger people shows that he has considerable good sense. He's just not willing to be pushed the way he doesn't want to go. So, far from being "unhealthy" I reckon he's got a very healthy will of his own. I'd leave him alone, if I were you. Time will resolve all your anxieties anyway. If he retains these same friends for another five years, they'll be 19 and 21. And that's a neligible age difference, isn't it? And incidentally did it never occur to you that the age of these friends of his, like the age of his brother's friends, could be unimportant anyway? They could be amusing, witty, sensitive, clever people with whom he feels comfortable? There's more to personality than age, you know. People who are great to know when they're middle aged were likely to have been as much fun in their childhoods, and people who are boring at 30 were much the same at 13.

I'm always a bit irritated by parents who say accusingly to their young people, "You care more about your friends than you do about us, your family!" as though that were a bad thing. Because, in fact, it's right and normal to seem to care more about making and keeping friends.

First, because you don't have to work so hard at making and keeping relations; you're born with them. All that you need to do is work at being happy with them — and you're halfway there in the average family because they care for you, and love you, and usually co-operate with you. Friends, on the other hand, you have to go and get for yourself. Strangers have to be met, and selected, and then talked to, and eventually persuaded to regard you as a likeable person.

Secondly, friends are the source of tomorrow's families. Unless you have social contacts, make acquaintances and then turn them into friends, you haven't a hope in hell of meeting a future life partner and having children of your own.

So, friends *are* more important than families, though you don't care less for your relations just because you care a lot for your friends. Love and involvement and compassion and companionship don't come in half pound packets like tea, in a limited quantity. They bubble up from the bottomless pit of your emotions; the more people you have to love and share experiences with the more love and sharing you have to give.

Definitions

But, what *is* a friend? It's a word that has changed its meaning over the years. In the nineteenth century, people spoke of their relatives — even their parents — as their friends. The word meant just "those people who care about me". Today we tend to use it to mean almost all the people we know *apart* from our relations.

You'll find it easier to understand your social contacts, however, if you tidy up your definitions.

COLLEAGUE. Someone you work with, either at a job, or in school or college (ie. schoolmate) or in any special activity — like being on a committee. You may not like a colleague but have to stay "friendly" with them so that you can work together.

ACQUAINTANCE. Someone you know slightly. You don't feel strongly about them one way or another.

ORDINARY FRIENDS. People you know fairly well, and definitely like. Often people with whom you've grown up — so they're almost part of the scenery. Sometimes there's a crowd or gang of you.

CLOSE FRIENDS. People you know well and care a lot about. You confide in them more than with ordinary friends — and can depend on them.

BEST FRIEND. Usually there is only one of these (although you can have two or more friends as level best). The feeling you have for them is much closer to love than liking. You share everything — good or bad — and however much you may argue, they remain your best friend.

If you look at the list carefully, you'll see at once that you can't expect the same reaction from all of them. Yet surprisingly often young people do have such expectations.

Some complain that they are "unpopular" when what they mean is that not all their colleagues think they're the cat's pyjamas.

Others say they have "no friends" when what they mean is that they treat all the people they know as acquaintances and then are miserable because those people don't respond to them as friends.

And some complain they have "hardly any friends" when what they mean is that they have the normal couple of close friends and one best friend, and want all their ordinary friends to be the same.

It is important to be realistic — to understand what friendship is truly about and adjust your social activities accordingly, improving them where necessary.

I MEET LOTS OF PEOPLE BUT I HAVE NO REAL FRIENDS—WHY?

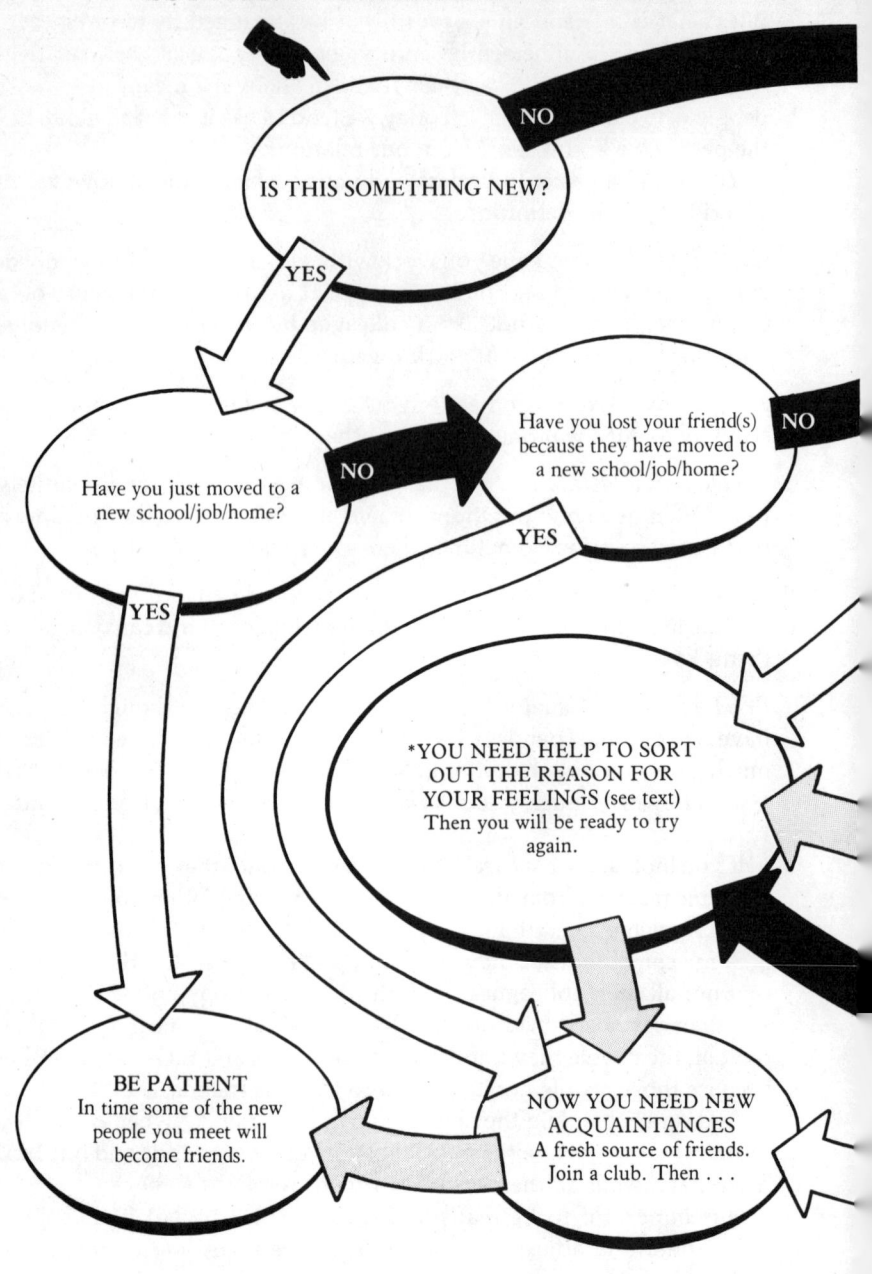

IS THIS SOMETHING NEW?

- NO →
- YES ↓

Have you just moved to a new school/job/home?

- NO → **Have you lost your friend(s) because they have moved to a new school/job/home?**
  - NO →
  - YES ↓
- YES ↓

*YOU NEED HELP TO SORT OUT THE REASON FOR YOUR FEELINGS (see text) Then you will be ready to try again.

BE PATIENT In time some of the new people you meet will become friends.

NOW YOU NEED NEW ACQUAINTANCES A fresh source of friends. Join a club. Then . . .

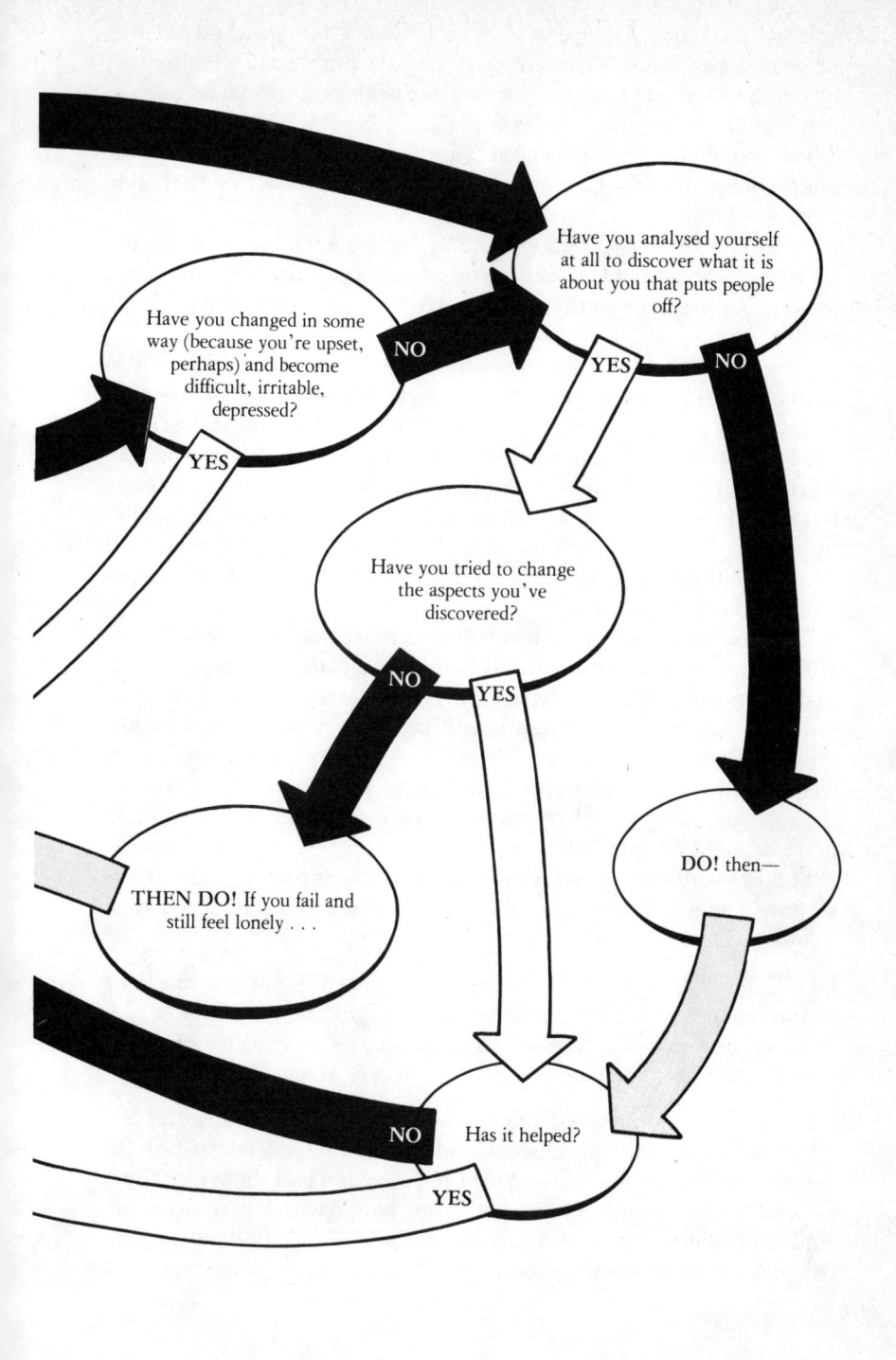

- Have you analysed yourself at all to discover what it is about you that puts people off?
- Have you changed in some way (because you're upset, perhaps) and become difficult, irritable, depressed?
- Have you tried to change the aspects you've discovered?
- THEN DO! If you fail and still feel lonely . . .
- DO! then—
- Has it helped?

This flowchart will help people who are going through a bad patch as far as making friends is concerned to solve the problem for themselves, by being willing to make an effort and work at getting to know people.

It will also help those people who can't solve the problem for themselves by showing them they need to seek help — and you'll notice that one section of the chart has an asterisk against it. The section that says, "You need help —"

What sort of help? The guidance of someone who is sympathetic, understanding and able to show you how to open doors to your own mind and behaviour so that you can be more comfortable with other people.

This sort of help is called *counselling*. It can be offered by social workers, or teachers or by people at the various special young people's help centres there are around (see the Information Section at the end of the book), but also by any sensible, sympathetic adult. A parent can do it for you, if you'll let them — which means listening to what they have to say and accepting and acting on their suggestions. However, many young people feel they can't take this sort of guidance from parents, and need an outsider's cooler view — which is why the special counsellors have a lot going for them.

The flowchart will be of less value to those very uptight self-conscious people who can't cope with making acquaintances, let alone making friends. Their problems may run more deeply, and be based on a lack of self-esteem (because it will be obvious that until you like yourself, and can be your own friend there's no way you're going to be a friend to others) and acute crippling shyness. They need help with life as a whole, and not just with friendships, and I will consider their needs in more detail in Chapter 7.

But for everyone else, let me repeat a set of facts that should be clear by now, and which, if you would be a friend-blessed person, you must not forget.

FACT ONE. Friendship is a rope with two ends. It is not possible to be connected to a person who isn't connected to you. So, you have to give as much as you want to get in a friendship — tolerance, affection, humour, concern and everything else you care about.

FACT TWO. People change all the time. A person can be cheerful and interested in you in the morning, miserable and interested only in herself in the afternoon. *You do the same*. So, don't take it personally if a friend is at some time or other not all you would wish him or her to be. And remember, when you're having one of your own bad patches, do tell your friends that is why you're being such a drag — that it isn't that you've gone off them. And encourage them to be as honest with you. That way there'll be fewer rows.

FACT THREE. Friendship, even best friendship, should not be totally exclusive. If your best friend shows he or she has other close friends, don't jump to the conclusion that you are any the less important because your friend has room in his life for others. Sharing does not necessarily mean losing out.

FACT FOUR. Generally speaking, friendship has to be worked for. There are some people in the world who are so charming, lovable and generally marvellous that they attract friends as a clover field draws bees. *They are rare.* Most of us have to put a lot of effort into being warm and interesting and attractive. The more you try — as long as you don't make the recipients of your efforts feel guilty about you, that is — the more you will be rewarded with friendship.

FACT FIVE. The way you look and dress may be the first point at which you connect with others, but that doesn't mean that it's the only part of you that matters. It's your mind and spirit that make people feel they can warm their hands at you.

FACT SIX. Finding, making and keeping friends means putting yourself out, going to places you may not expect to enjoy, doing things that bore you — making way for others' needs.

Other people's behaviour

One of the stages through which you pass as you convert an acquaintance into a friend, of whatever degree, is recognising aspects of that person's behaviour which are unattractive and unlikeable, and either accepting them as part of the total package which is that person, or, if possible, helping them to recognise the faulty bits and change them.

It is also helpful to identify such behaviour in yourself.

Quite a number of things people do to muck up their relationships can be tracked down to three basic causes.

(Well, perhaps four, if you include the possibility that someone is just plain nasty — and there are, sadly, a few like that in the world. People who actually enjoy cruelty and harshness, and are quite content with themselves however many others they make unhappy. And when you try to find a reason for it — sad childhood experience, or pain at others' hands in any way — you just can't. With people like that it's probably best to keep as far away from them as possible.)

Here is a list of the bad behaviour of the sort that makes people unlikeable.

The things people do

BULLYING. They push others around. They use their physical size and strength to force others to do what they want. They terrorise the shy, the quiet, anyone on their own. They like to use blackmail — threatening to do damage unless they get what they want, be it sweets or sex.

LYING. They tell tall tale after tall tale. And even when they are found out as pathetic liars — which they always are — they go on spinning their yarns.

CRUELTY. They are unkind for the sheer joy of it. They spoil your property, hit you, and hurt you. Not for any reward — they just seem to enjoy it.

SNEAKING. They run to parents/teachers/bosses with every scrap of tittle-tattle they can. They watch others secretly, read private letters and diaries.

STANDOFFISHNESS. They just don't respond to others. Speak to them and they shrug or turn away. Invite them to join in and they never do.

USING. They get something for themselves out of every contact. A pretty girl makes a great buddy of a plain one — just to use her as a foil and make herself look even prettier. Or a person with a lively personality and lots of fun in his/her life who doesn't want to bother to work at school makes a friend of a quiet, shy, swotting type just in order to use him/her to do his school work for him.

STIRRING. They go from one person to another, telling tales, creating bad feelings by saying things like, "Joe said you were a bore —" and then telling Joe you said he was a louse — and generally making waves on otherwise smooth ponds.

PUSHINESS. They join in on everything, invited or not. When two people are talking privately, the pusher comes thrusting in. They volunteer for anything and everything and no one ever gets a look in if they can get there first.

SWANKING. They show off all the time — about their clothes, their friends, their clever relations, their exam marks, everything you can think of. They sound very like liars, though they aren't necessarily embroidering the truth — they're just making sure that absolutely everyone knows how superior they are in every way.

SULKERS AND SHOUTERS. They fly into a passion when things don't go their way — either refusing to talk to anyone in so spectacular fashion that their silence is deafening, or screaming insults and generally creating aggro.

That's just my list — it may well be that you can add others to it. If so, do so.

And then, see if you can work out *why* people show this sort of behaviour.

There are, I believe, just three basic causes for all of it.

1   LACK OF SELF-ESTEEM
2   INSECURITY
3   BAD TRAINING

And well, maybe that fourth one — sheer inborn nastiness. But as I believe it to be rare, let's leave that to one side at present.

LACK OF SELF-ESTEEM means simply that a person doesn't like him/herself. As you'll see in Chapter 7, there can be lots of reasons for this, and it is something that can be dealt with — people can cure themselves of the problem.

INSECURITY means never really feeling safe in your world. We all need to be loved by people we can trust — to feel sure that the pattern of our lives will always be there to make invisible but protective walls. Knowing that your breakfast will be there when you wake up in the morning, that there's your own familiar roof to cover you when you go to bed at night, is vital. And so is knowing that the people you love, love you.

Sadly, not all parents are as good as they might be at giving young people this sense of security. Often just because they don't know how much babies and children need to be shown love, they bring up their teenagers to feel unloved. The result in some cases is lack of self-esteem; in others it's insecurity; in lots it's an unhappy mixture of the two.

BAD TRAINING is what it sounds like — never being taught how to be aware of other people and their needs. A much-loved child who is wrapped in his parents' concern and who is given masses of security may, unfortunately, also be given the idea that he is the centre of the universe around whom everyone else revolves. That's how it is in his family, he reasons, so that is how it will be outside. When such a person goes into the big wide world and finds that the universe is revolving very happily, thank you, round all sorts of other people, he just can't handle the fact. He has to learn — sometimes painfully — to take his place with all the others there are who are of equal importance to him, though he never knew they existed.

Now, look again at that list of ten pieces of disagreeable behaviour. Take a look at people you know who display them.

And then try to work out, based on what you know of their lives, from what they have said, and what others have told you, what might be the cause of it.

But remember always that behaviour can be paradoxical.

That is, people sometimes do the very opposite you'd expect them to do logically. For example, a person who is desperate for affection and friendship, having been starved of it and feeling very insecure as a result, may bully — behaviour which makes others feel very unfriendly indeed. He does it because he doesn't know any other way to behave; after all, it's probably all he's been shown at home (parents often teach their children to be bullies by bullying them).

Which means that the best way to cure a bully is not to shun him *but to be friendly*.

This does not mean giving in to blackmail.

If a bully tries to force you to part with money or whatever under threat of personal violence, you stand up to him — if needs be collecting other people who are your friends to help you do so — or by telling parents, teachers or bosses what is happening. That isn't sneaking — it's plain commonsense.

But next time you're having a few friends round, *ask the bully too*. In time you should be able to get past his nasty front and, slowly, teach him that the way to make friends and influence people is to be warm, not horrible.

I'm not pretending it's easy to do — or that you will necessarily succeed. But it's a strategy well worth trying.

Use the same techniques for others who are behaving paradoxically. The pusher needs to be invited to join in things if he is to learn to be less pushy. The user has to be used by others to realise how disagreeable a way it is to behave.

And, if after every attempt at understanding the root of a person's bad behaviour all you come up with is that he's a plain bad person, then as I've said, the only answer is to give him a wide berth. Poor devil.

To sum up:

People who lack SELF-ESTEEM need to be shown they are likeable, to be given attention and praise and respect.

People who are INSECURE need lots of reassurance that you can be trusted.

A person who has simply experienced BAD TRAINING can be taught to behave better by having his unpleasant behaviour treated with cool disdain, and his better behaviour rewarded with warm approval.

Of course, if you recognise some of these forms of behaviour in yourself, you're the best person to cure yourself of it, aren't you? Realise why you're doing it and work out for yourself what effect the behaviour has on others. It's really as easy as that.

CHAPTER SEVEN
YOU AND YOUR PROBLEMS

I long ago realised that there is no such thing as a truly carefree person. Everybody, the most brilliant, the most beautiful, the most talented, the most rich, has problems. And everyone cares a great deal about them; some may not show how much on the surface, but that doesn't mean they don't care. They do, like the very devil.

If I could have discovered this vital fact at the age of twelve or thirteen I could have saved myself a great deal of anguish. I could have avoided those umpteen nights of falling asleep on a sodden pillow, after spending hours weeping miserably over how I looked, how I sounded, how I behaved . . . I could have got on with making the most of what I had rather than the least of what I had not.

You are a much nicer, and better person than you think you are.

This is true even of people who swagger about and show off and make pests of themselves by being very conceited indeed. Conceited behaviour is rarely born of a genuine sense of self worth, but is the very opposite; because a person has a deep down feeling of being awful, he or she tries to kid himself, and others, that really he's a *marvellous* person and puts on a show accordingly. It's tragedy when this happens, of course, because conceited people are so very hard to like that they tend to be shunned and therefore become ever more convinced they're a hopeless case, and even more conceited in behaviour as a result. It's called over-compensation, and it's very boring and very sad when it happens.

Why do people get such a bad notion of themselves? Is it born into humans all over the world? Or is it something we're taught?

Some of it, I think, is inborn — our feelings of inadequacy probably have evolved, like the rest of us, from primitive man's first faltering steps in the world.

But more important than this inborn sense of weakness is the way children are brought up in this country, and many others. For a very long time now children have been seen by adults as creatures which have to be trained and guided and pushed and manipulated into "good" behaviour. It has been taken for granted that childish behaviour — such as being explorative and noisy and interested in your own physical needs and the feelings you get from your own body — is badness that has to be stamped out and replaced with adult conformity.

Side by side with this adult passion for control of childish behaviour there is a fear of giving praise for childish achievement. How many adults ever say to young children, "Aren't you clever!" "Aren't you beautiful!" "Aren't you nice!" They might think it — indeed they often do. But they hardly ever say it for fear of "spoiling" the child.

Instead, whatever the child does that they like, they urge him or her to do it more and more by *diminishing* what he has already done.

"Second in the class," says Dad, busting with pride and biting it back. "Not bad — next time make it first."

We bring up our children by putting them down.

We're getting a little better, mind you. Today's adults are at last realising that a scrap of praise beats a ton of criticism hands down for getting the effect you want. But there still remain large numbers of people in their teens and older who are bedevilled by self-dislike and self-consciousness, who find life much more complicated than it need be as a result.

If your problem is lack of self-esteem, how can you solve it?

Blushing and sweating and trembling

First, let's consider the physical reactions some people get to their lack of self-esteem.

There are people who suffer a great deal from a number of physical reactions ranging through blushing, restlessness, rapid heartbeat, a feeling of nausea, diarrhoea, sweating of hands, feet and body, especially armpits, and assorted aches and pains. These reactions make it difficult if not impossible for them to go out and about, to meet people and build any sort of social life and may in some cases even prevent them from going to school or work.

Their problem is the adrenalin response. As you will recall from Chapter I the human body is governed largely by chemical messengers called hormones. They have a large number of functions to do with growth and development, activity and food usage and many other aspects of daily living. An important hormone is *adrenalin*, called sometimes the "FIGHT-OR-FLIGHT" hormone.

Imagine you are walking down a hill, and that there is a heavy lorry at the top of the hill. Suddenly the lorry goes out of control and starts to veer towards you at full tilt, rocking from side to side.

You need to do one of two things. Either to fight off the threat — perhaps by jumping into the lorry's cab as it reaches you and putting on the brake, or, more probably, running like the devil to get out of its way. Fight it, or fly from it.

In order to do either, you need to use your muscles very powerfully, and to do that, your muscles need a lot of extra food, and extra oxygen, the fuel which powers them. Also, the messages that come from the brain to make the muscles work must travel extremely rapidly if your response to the threatening lorry is to be in time to be of any use.

So, as you see and hear the lorry, your brain processes the messages coming in, identifies "Threat" and sends an urgent signal to the adrenal glands to pump out their messenger hormone, adrenalin. This acts in seconds on the muscle fibres of heart and blood vessels, resulting in a greatly increased rate of beating and engorgement of the blood vessels, so that the food-and-oxygen-rich blood is sent pumping rapidly all over the body, where it will be needed to deal with the lorry.

At the same time, blood has to be redirected from non-essential work to distant muscles which will be working hardest. So an initial enlarging of surface blood vessels, which causes reddening of the face, gives way to tightening of them, which leads to pallor.

All this extra activity results in increased activity of the surface sweat glands — first a "hot" sweat as the surface of the body reddens, then a cold one as blood retreats to fight/flight muscles leaving the skin damp and chilled.

The oxygen supply has to be increased too, because the lungs need more air, so breathing rates speed up. The gut, from which food supplies are drawn, also has to go into overdrive, as the smooth muscle walls react to the adrenalin, and this causes crampy feelings of nausea, and, obviously, diarrhoea as food is shoved hurriedly along the system.

And as the messages come thick and fast to the fight/flight muscles they become tense with stored-up action. You are ready to jump at the right moment and deal with that lorry.

All of this preparation, after it has done its job, takes time to die down. Long after the lorry has disappeared at the bottom of the hill leaving you behind safe and sound, or long after you've been a hero and stopped it, your body will show adrenalin reaction. The pale face, the sweating, the belly cramps, the rapid heart beat and breathing rates — and also trembling as the muscles gradually lose their special tightness.

If you've ever had a nasty fright, you'll recognise all these feelings, will know how long they can hang on leaving you feeling worn out and low. And you'll have understood it's all a normal reaction.

But suppose you get such reactions when there is no lorry at the top of the hill? When the only threat around is of standing up in class to read a bit of work aloud, or walking into a room where there are people you don't know well, or talking to someone you like the look of? When you get those feelings — shaking and sweating and reddening and bellyache — you feel like an ass. You also feel thoroughly uncomfortable and want to avoid getting the feelings again. So you regularly dodge standing up in class, going into rooms full of people you don't know, or talking to people you like the look of.

This is what happens to people who have poor self-esteem.

They have been trained to think themselves so useless and awful that everything they encounter — even ordinary things — is seen as a threat, something to fight off or fly from. *Mostly fly from because self-haters never believe they can fight off anything.*

Another trouble with the adrenalin reaction is that it is self-fuelling. The person who gets it and uses it — and fights off the worry — gets some benefit from all that physical preparation. The reward they get from having made an effort helps them find the adrenalin feelings less nasty, and so they get over the reaction more quickly. But people who don't use it suffer the shaking and all the rest of it, get no reward, and build in an added fear. *The fear of being frightened.*

Which is why it is essential to force yourself, however painful it is, to deal with an adrenalin response positively.

STRATEGY
for fright

1. Accept the fact that these very physical reactions *are not a sign of illness*. Some people are convinced they have some dreadful heart disease or lung disease because of it all. YOU HAVE NOT. It all starts in your mind and it's a normal response, if rather exaggerated.

2. When you are in a situation which makes you have the reaction — reddening, then going

white, trembling, breathing fast — try to look at yourself in a mirror. *You will see that there is nothing much to look at that is different.* You are not as red as you feel or sweating as much as you think.

It is important to remember that what you are feeling is much greater than what you are showing. *Unless you draw attention to the state you're in, very few people will actually notice.*

3   Refuse to give in to the temptation to turn and run away from whatever the situation is. You want to dodge standing up in class? MAKE YOURSELF PUT YOUR HAND UP. No, it won't be easy. But do it. *Ignore the way you feel*. Let the redness happen, let the sweat pour, let your voice tremble. You'll come to no harm from any of it. *You can cope.*

4   Do it again. And again. You'll find it will get easier each time.

5   Now you have proved to yourself you can do one thing that frightens you, start on another alarming area. *Keep on repeating your efforts*. You won't get rid of your excess adrenalin reaction with one blow of your trusty confidence sword — but you can, very slowly, build up your self-confidence by actually doing what it is you most fear.

6   Don't kid yourself that you've got rid of your fear for ever, just because you've overcome it a few times. You haven't. It will always be there waiting for you — but it won't matter, because you've proved you can overcome the unpleasant effects of adrenalin, and use the positive ones.

> 7   Look around for someone who is suffering as you used to before you set out to get rid of your fear of fear. And offer to help him or her do as you have done — giving lots of encouragement. Not only will you help the other person — you'll lift your own self-confidence a dozen notches. Helping others cope with something you've already coped with makes you feel marvellous. This is not "using" a person — it's enlightened self-interest. It helps you both.

There are people who do not get physical reactions to their lack of self-esteem, but still feel lousy inside because they believe they are so ugly/short/tall/skinny/spotty or whatever. They spend much of their time, if not all of it, looking at everyone else's good points and comparing them with their own bad ones. No wonder they always come to the conclusion that they haven't a hope in hell of making happy relationships.

How can you learn to like yourself better?

What you *don't* do is embark on the comparison game. If you think you're ugly, some people say, look around for someone who is uglier than you are and gloat over their awfulness to give yourself a lift. If you've got ten spots, look for someone with eleven to sneer at.

This is a bad strategy:

Because it always kicks back. Sure, you can find someone uglier, spottier or whatever than yourself to despise — but you'll always see at the same time someone lovelier and smoother to envy.

A much better strategy is to assess your own *good* aspects and balance them with the aspects of yourself you don't like. (Note I didn't say "bad" aspects — it isn't bad to be ugly/short/tall/skinny/spotty etcetera. It's just uncomfortable if you don't like being that way.) Then deal with the things you don't like in a practical way.

There are some things that undoubtedly can be modified in some way: people who are "too fat" can diet and get thinner. People who are "too thin" can eat more to try to get fatter. Both need to beware of getting too anxious about what they eat, however; people can make themselves severely ill if they think about diet and food too much (see Chapter I).

Those things that can't be altered — like an inborn tendency to plumpness/thinness and being taller/shorter than is average can be lived with if you learn to use them positively, and use various tricks of clothing and, where relevant, make-up to disguise them.

In *a few* cases stronger methods may be needed to deal with the problems — but do note they are few and far between. Plastic surgery, for example, has a genuinely useful role for a person who has really big sticking-out ears — it is not the remedy for someone who would simply rather have a different shaped nose (unless it really is awful).

The chart on pages 124—5 will show you how to deal with the problems — and if your special one isn't here, it does not mean that it is incredibly unique and that you are supremely cursed. It only means that there just isn't room to put in every single thing people fret about. It could also mean that it is really so small a problem that it doesn't merit inclusion. You can, with a little thought, fill in the column headings for such items by studying the answers to the problems that *are* listed.

The basic strategy for dealing with physical aspects of yourself that you dislike should now be clear.

You change what you can, disguise what you can't, and then tell yourself that there is no way you're going to spend your life fretting over something you're stuck with.

And although I've already said that the comparison game is odious, there's a lot to be said for old-fashioned blessing-counting which is quite different. "I may have a less than beautiful nose, but I've got beautiful eyes — " can be a cheering thought.

By no means all the problems people in their teens have in dealing with their world can be covered by finding ways of coping with anxiety and shyness, or by coming to terms with physical "shortcomings". You will often find yourself wanting to kick yourself because you think you've made a fool of yourself by saying the wrong thing to the wrong person at the wrong time, or because you've chickened out on an opportunity, or because you've been given an opportunity but were too daft to recognise it and so let it slip through your fingers.

There is nothing I or anyone else can do to help you with situations like that. They are an inevitable part of experience, of growing into your world, and if you could avoid all such hazards and difficulties at your age you'd be a miracle. You'd also be a bit of a bore, one of those totally self-confident, totally capable, totally knowing types who are acceptable when they're fifty or sixty (after all, they've had time to learn!) but repellent at sixteen.

It's important you give yourself permission to be imperfect. Too often young people set themselves impossible standards of behaviour, achievement, excitement, ability, everything. They try to reach those standards, inevitably they can't because they are unreachable, and then hate themselves as "failures". *They are not*. They've just been unrealistic.

So learn to set yourself only achievable goals, one at a time. The shy person who says to himself, "Today I'll talk to the girl I see every morning at the bus stop", and then a month later says to himself, "Today I will ask that girl I talk to every morning at the bus stop to come out with me", has every chance of making it. The one who says, "From today on, I'm going to be the brightest, most cheerful talker in the world, and chat up every girl I meet and ask 'em all out", hasn't a hope.

Danger areas

Having said in effect that being unsure of yourself and less than perfect in your own eyes need not damage your life, I must now point out that there is a sense in which you are vulnerable if you feel this way.

You are easy prey to other people's manipulations.

Fashion

The most common of the manipulators are the fashion-mongers. Those who imply that unless you wear *these* clothes, listen to *this* music, go to *that* concert you're an outsider — a no-good, a bore. If you can afford to do all these things, great. You won't actually *be* the opposite of a no-good, a bore, an outsider, but at least you'll think you are.

But suppose you can't be a dedicated follower of fashion and your family, who are the source of your income, can't afford to help you be one? If you're one of the people who are unsure of themselves and shy, this can feel like a nail in your coffin and make you even more depressed than you are.

Try to see fashion for what it is. On one level, it's just fun; a way of decking yourself to be amusing, or pretty, or both. But on another it's something much more important and potentially damaging to you: it is a major industry, making a lot of money for a lot of people by manipulating the self-doubts of young people (older ones too, come to that). It is in the interests of the money-men to make you feel desperately unhappy if your clothes and records and all the rest of it aren't changed every week or so. *And you can resist their pressures once you realise they are there.*

The best way is to seek out a "look" of your own, one designed to suit you as you are, rather than to make you look like a carbon copy of everyone else. Both boys and girls need to look appraisingly at their

124 *Growing Pains*

PROBLEM	DIRECT ACTION	COMPENSATION
Tallness	Nil	Wear flat shoes, making sure you adapt current fashion. Tallness is usually a girl's anxiety, but they are fortunate because they can develop a distinctive fashion "look".
Shortness	Nil	Wear high heels. Men's shoes now are easy to get with three to four inch heels (and this is most often a boy's anxiety).
Plumpness	Diet. *Check first* with doctor/school counsellor that it is necessary. If you are of good average weight but bulkier in some areas than others, then see next columns. (For good diet see p. 29, for slimming clubs p. 190.)	Wear hair set wide round a plump face — reduces size of face. Choose subtle colours for clothes. Make sure clothes fit well; better one size too big than one too tight. No over-tight belts or sweaters etc.
Thinness	Check diet. Eating enough? Check with doctor or school counsellor. May need to increase food intake.	Pull hair well back from thin face. Choose bright strong colours, and again well-fitting clothes.
Spottiness	See pages 35–6	Nil
Big Nose	None	You probably have other good strong features, such as big eyes, good cheekbones.
Protruding Teeth	*See Dentist*	No need for this — can be treated by dentist — may take time but well worth the wearing of braces to improve dental appearance.
Big Ears	Nil	Often goes with good strong features.

You and Your Problems   125

DISGUISE	CORRECTION	UNALTERABLE?
When choosing your fashion, look at all-over straight lines which elongate you. Cross stripes are good, up and down are not. Opt for a curvy line — it shortens. Very tall boys need squared-off shoulders, bulky sweaters etc. for same effect.	Nil	Yes
Always make sure clothes are the right length. Even an inch too long makes you look dumpy (opt for strong jazzy colours — adds to your impact).	Nil	Yes
Girls can use make-up to shape face — local beauty shop will show how. Boys can, as soon as possible, grow a beard — easy to shape to your body.	In a few rare cases may be a medical problem. See doctor.	Sometimes yes
Soft fabrics worn bunched add bulk. Tight belts make most of slender effect but bulk out hips and chest.	In a few rare cases may be a medical problem. See doctor.	Sometimes yes
Use Covermark — good for both sexes.	Medical problem, see doctor.	Sometimes yes
Haircuts by experts can much improve balance of profile. Spend most you can afford at top stylists.	If really severe plastic surgery. See doctor.	No
No need. See previous column.	See previous column.	No
Cover with good hairstyle.	If really severe plastic surgery. See doctor.	No

overall appearance and to decide what they like to look like, and then to use what cash they have to equip themselves accordingly. And if the look they come up with is wildly different from everyone else's, so what?

Mind Benders

More worrying than fashion-mongering is ideas-mongering. In recent years more and more cults have developed which depend on recruiting new people in ever increasing numbers. Some of them are religious in concept. Some are political. Some are a mixture of both. Many of them demand of their new members money, and much more sinister, an abandonment of family, of school work, of old friends and interests.

Beware of them.

I'm not saying that all religious or political conversions are a bad thing. Many people are genuinely convinced of the ideals and aims of various groups and join them of their own free will. But it *is* a bad thing if you have to be coaxed to join.

Those sorts of cults which take novices off for weekend visits to special centres where they are bombarded with propaganda, those cults which operate by picking up young people in the street and inviting them to "a friendly supper" where they then push their beliefs at them, are the ones to treat with extreme caution.

Remember always that the established religions usually make it difficult for new people to enter them. To become an orthodox Jew, a practising Catholic or a communicant of the Church of England, for example, you have to undergo a course of instruction and be assessed for your suitability. By the time you belong you've had lots of time to think and have been encouraged to be *sure* it's what you want. The persuasive cults don't operate this way.

Ask yourself what the cults are offering you? Have the good sense to check out their beliefs with your friends, your family or anyone else whose opinions you trust before jumping in the deep end.

And the same applies to political systems of belief which tell you that as long as you do things *their* way, tomorrow will be perfect. Never mind if it means violence, lying, intolerance of opposing ideas today — the ends will justify the means.

This is not true.

One of the reasons for the attraction of some extreme political ideas is that they offer a sense of togetherness against a hostile world. When you look about you and see injustice, or cruelty or selfishness, and a lot of people who have something you haven't and want to have, then you feel isolated, angry, frustrated. If someone then comes along and offers you a scapegoat for all these bad things you see, and all these bad feelings you have, and tells you that getting rid of the bosses and having a workers' revolution — or getting rid of the blacks, the Jews, the Catholics or whoever — will leave more room at the top for you, it is all too easy to be beguiled. Especially if the message is wrapped around with secrecy and demands a bit of cloak-and-daggerism to arrange meetings. It turns it all into a most entrancing, if dangerous, game. It's even more attractive if older people show disapproval.

So, my political message is that there is always danger in totalitarian ideas with oversimplified answers, whether they belong to the extreme left or the extreme right of politics. I'm not saying that the only worthwhile ideas are those that straddle the middle ground, the pale pink or pale blue sugared-almond brand of political thought. I'm just warning you that it is all too easy to be sold a false dream by people who are unscrupulous and manipulative for their own selfish ends. Be as suspicious and as questioning of all political ideas as you are of all others that are handed to you; ask yourself always why you find the ideas attractive, and take your time deciding if you want to share them.

Take your time before you join anything. If it's worth joining at all, it will still be there a year or more from now, after you've had the chance to think it through and develop a little more understanding.

Drugs

These include alcohol, tobacco, marijuana (pot, grass, etc.), amphetamine (speed), solvents (glue, cleaning fluid), heroin and cocaine.

Some of them are legal — alcohol and tobacco — but that does not necessarily mean they are safe to use.

The hard fact is that tobacco is a proven cause of illness and premature death not only from cancer (and lung cancer is a particularly nasty way to die) but also from heart disease and stroke, neither of which are at all agreeable or romantic experiences.

Alcohol used in small quantities is a temporary stimulant which then acts also as a depressant, and used in larger quantities can do a lot of damage to liver, blood vessels, eyes, gut and a whole range of other body tissues, as well as damaging the ability to think, work and to have a satisfactory sex life.

The other drugs are illegal, and many of them carry definite health hazards similar to those of tobacco and alcohol as well as the risk of penalties involving fines and/or imprisonment.

Add it all together and these drugs are not good news. So why do people use them?

Because at the beginning of their use, they're fun. They make your brain a bit woozy, the sort of dizzy feeling you get on a roller-coaster, and may create a state called euphoria: a sense of great well-being, a conviction that the world you live in is the most delightful, amusing, comfortable place there can be, and that you are its most witty and beautiful inhabitant.

Euphoria is a great feeling, while it lasts. It lasts a very short time and is always followed by a depression in which the world is clearly lousy, hateful and miserably uncomfortable, and you personally are its dreariest and unhappiest inhabitant.

Since the depression is so much nastier than the euphoria and lasts so much longer, people afflicted with it are all too likely to seek another dose of whatever it was that gave them the euphoria — forgetting or refusing to remember that the same stuff also caused the reactive depression. They use the drug, get the euphoria *for a shorter time* and a resulting depression *for a longer time*.

They then tend to use the drug in greater quantities in order to prolong the euphoria — and with it the depression, of course — and so in time become hooked. They live a dismal pattern of short euphoria, prolonged depression and of course all the attendant physical and emotional damage that goes with the drug.

It would be a lie to say this happens to everyone. There are people who can take the occasional beer or glass of wine or whatever and enjoy it, cope well with the let-down that follows the lift-up and don't get hooked. Good luck to them.

The trouble is, when you're young you can't know for sure whether you're the sort of person who can handle a drug this way. You may be the sort who is vulnerable — getting much worse depressions than most people after the use of the drug and therefore likely to abuse the stuff thereafter. It's safer, in the long run, therefore, to take a very long time to establish your own pattern of alcohol use.

If you find you're tempted to take more than you really know you should — and every one of us knows how much is right, if we listen to our own inner reactions — then for heaven's sake, *lay off*. You need time to learn how to use the stuff well.

As for the illegal drugs — they're *illegal* and that's all about it. You can't live in a society without laws — they protect as well as control you — so unless you really want to make big troubles for yourself, you'll dodge illegal actions. Especially when, as in this case, they're unhealthy as well.

And as an ex-nurse I *know* how unhealthy they are. I've looked after people who have been ruined by the use of heroin. People so thin, so bedraggled, so runny-nosed, red-rimmed about the eyes, so covered in sores and infected needle wounds, so racked with diarrhoea and vomiting, so twisted with belly cramps, so *ill* that I wanted to weep for them. And I've actually wept for the ones whose bodies I had to prepare for the undertaker, some of them younger than I was myself at the time — in my twenties. I know we've all got to die sometime, but this is one of the most disgusting ways to do it that I know.

Some started simply because they were bored; some got swept into the drug scene because they hadn't the will-power to avoid "metooism"; and some were just curious. They wanted to know what it felt like to be "high", to get excited, to see things through distorted vision. And they paid a heavy price for it.

So, there are truly good personal as well as legal reasons for not using drugs — including long-term ones (there is increasing evidence that glue and solvent sniffing affects chromosomes, the body structures that carry on the genetic information needed to make new life. In other words, these substances may, in later life, cause cancer in the individual who used them, and also lead to the birth of damaged babies. This isn't proven but it seems very likely). Only a fool denies these reasons.

And the fact that some adults cheat like the devil and sit there with a cigarette in one hand and a glass of whisky in the other telling *you* you mustn't use drugs, doesn't alter the fact that you'd be better off if you didn't. They may go in for double-think — but maddening though that is, it isn't a good enough reason to go ahead and be as stupid as they are.

Lawbreaking

There are more ways of behaving illegally than drug abuse. There's shoplifting and window-breaking and bashing up phone boxes and train seats and all the rest of it.

This sort of behaviour is often performed as part of a gang's activities. The evidence is that not many people go around all on their own cutting up train seats, although shoplifters often act on their own, of course.

It is unlikely in the extreme that people who go in for lawbreaking in a big way are a) interested in reading a book like this and b) prepared to consider anything I might have to say on the subject. But anyone who thinks that destroying a phone box is fun when it could be the only way some people have of calling an ambulance in a hurry; or that stealing from shops is okay because they're insured; or that ruining state property is acceptable because the state treats some of its citizens unfairly; ought to think again.

Because it is a lousy thing to do. And the people who do it wouldn't like it if it happened to them.

But I can say this much to some people — those who really share my views about the general lousiness of this sort of activity, but who get swept into it because "all their friends do it".

I know it can be painful to swim against this sort of tide, to be jeered at as chicken because you hang back. I know it can be lonely to leave behind a gang that is fun, on the grounds that you don't want to behave in the way they do when it comes to vandalism and robbery.

But in the long run, won't you be better off if you take these risks and turn your back on such a crowd?

That way you avoid the risk of getting nicked and going to court, even to approved school or prison, if you're old enough. Over to you.

Coping with school work

Many school people feel overwhelmed by the demands of their teachers. It seems to them that the teachers are dedicated to stuffing their heads with information they don't want, skills that are uninteresting, and ideas that are boring. But in fact education is something that comes not from the teacher to the pupil, but out of the pupil him or herself, with the teacher's aid to extract it. The very word means that — education comes from *educare*, a Latin word that means "to draw forth". So when a pupil battles with teacher to avoid learning, all he's doing is fighting with himself. He's preventing himself from getting any pleasure out of time that he *must* put in at school, and also adding to his burdens by making teachers irritable and hard to work with. He is also damaging his future prospects because people who don't work well at school often have added difficulty in finding work they can enjoy as much as they'd like to after they leave school.

Indeed, they have difficulty in finding work at all. The hard truth is that in times of high unemployment (approaching $3\frac{1}{2}$ million in the UK at the time of writing this) the people who find it hardest to get jobs are the unskilled, and school leavers who have never worked much and haven't a single exam qualification to show for their classroom years, are the least skilled of all. So it's simple self-preservation to work while you're at school, if you want to have a fighting chance of working at some sort of job after you leave it. Yes, there are people who have worked very hard indeed, who have pockets full of CSEs, 'O' levels, 'A' levels and even degrees who are unemployed — but they still have a better chance than people with no qualifications at all. Also, there is the hope that over the next few years a new pattern of employment will be created and job-finding will be easier. People who can remain at school, therefore, riding out these particularly bad years, could be better off than those who throw up their hands and stop trying to get an education.

The best way to cope with classroom work is to make sure you're up-to-date with what is being done. This may involve a period of hard revision, but it's worth making that effort. The best time to start is when exams are due; then the rest of the class is revising too, and you aren't in the awful situation of trying to learn old work while also trying to keep up with new work. If you use the following strategy, *and ask the teaching staff for help* whenever you hit a patch of work you don't fully understand or can't handle, you could surprise yourself at how respectable a showing you can make when the exams start. At the very least you'll go into them feeling the reassurance of having done some useful work; at best, you'll find you actually begin to enjoy the effort and get better results than you'd hoped for.

STRATEGY
for Revision

1 START EARLY. It is no use trying to kid yourself the exam dates will never come and then panicking two weeks before they start. The teachers will tell your class when to begin revising. *That is the time to begin.*

2 Make a timetable. Each individual will need his or her own. It all depends on what subjects you have to revise and the amount of time each needs. But here are some general tips.

   A) Set aside the same block of time each day of the week — depending on your other commitments. You won't have to give up everything in order to revise; you need some time out, too.

So, if your youth club meets on Wednesday and you play football or swim on Fridays, set aside three hours on Monday, Tuesday and Thursday, and only one on Wednesday and Friday.

Remember the weekends. Sleeping late on Sunday feels great, but getting up an hour earlier and putting in a couple of hours each Sunday morning feels even better.

B) Set yourself blocks of time within each day's allotment for each subject. Never spend longer than an hour on a subject; you'll get bored and less productive if you do.

C) Add a space to your timetable for a daily tear-off list. Each day, before you start your revision, write the list of what you are to do that day. As you finish each subject, tick it off on the list. This will give you added incentive.

D) Don't study for hours and hours on end. There's a limit to how much you can take in and the longer hours will do you no good, but make you extra tired and therefore dispirited.

E) Eat little and often while you are studying. Big meals make you sleepy, lack of food makes your concentration lag.

F) Don't drink too much coffee or coke — it doesn't make you more alert — it can make you edgy and unrelaxed and the key to successful revision is to be alert but definitely relaxed.

3   Once a week, share a study session with a fellow reviser *at the same level you are*.

You and Your Problems 133

> (Someone who is faster than you will make you feel inadequate, someone who is slower will hold you back.) Hear each other's learned material, discover any problems you need help with, swop research information and ideas. *Once a week is enough.* If you share revision too often you'll become too social and less productive.
>
> 4 Try to be tidy and organised. You'll find it makes life a lot easier — and you'll save a lot of time.

QUESTIONS

Question 1 "I am a 14-year-old girl and recently my parents split up. Before they split, I saw them fight and it really used to worry me. My father now lives alone and I live with my mother and two sisters. I cannot seem to talk to my mother. I know she is under a lot of stress financially. Last year she even tried to kill herself. She thinks I want to live with my father, but I don't; but I can't stay with her much longer. I'm so miserable. The thing I want most right now is to live with some people I know. They have two children of their own, but I'm fairly sure they would have me because I brought it up casually. I stayed with them once and I cried when I had to come home. They showed me what family life should be like. I think my mother loves me but I can't be sure because she never talks to me."

Answer The main reason you long to move in with these friends is not so much because you care for them; it's because you love your mum so much that you want to escape from the sight of her unhappiness. So, even if you did move out, you wouldn't be content. You'd be worrying too much about your mother.

I think what you must do is help your parents see that even though they have stopped being Mr. and Mrs. they are still Mum and Dad, and insist they get together and try to make arrangements for you and your sisters that will make you all happier.

Talk to a teacher at school you like and trust, and see if she can help you talk to your mum, and to your dad, to explain how distressed you are. Perhaps they don't realise how you feel. Children in your situation all too often hide their feelings as part of their attempts to protect their already unhappy parents. Well, you must stop hiding them, and talk them out. You're suffering as much by this split as they are. You're entitled to their consideration

Question 2   "I get so frightened. My mum had an operation for cancer of the breast, and I keep thinking she's going to die. I can't talk to her about that, can I? And my dad gets upset if I even mention the fact she had the operation. It's like they're pretending it never happened. The doctors said she was all right and no need to worry, but I think they're lying, though my mum looks as well as she ever did."

Answer   Your parents' way of handling this frightening bit of their lives — which is getting on with living and refusing to fret over your mother's illness — has a lot going for it. Cancer of the breast, like many other cancers, is very treatable these days, and there's a real chance the operation has done all that is necessary and your mother really is as well as she looks. And that's how they are thinking.

Yes, there is also the chance that the disease will come back and that some time in the future she will die of it. But we all die sooner or later, and to waste the life we have worrying about what might be in the future is daft — because there is no way anyone can know, and anyway, what difference would it make? You might be run over by a bus tomorrow on your way to school — but can you spend today worrying about that possibility? That is how your parents are thinking and it's no bad way.

This isn't to be unsympathetic to your fears. I know the sheer panic that can fill you at the thought that someone you love might die. It's dreadful — and your instinct to talk about it is right. When you do it's easier to live with it, and set it aside. But it wouldn't be fair to burden your parents with this — they have enough to cope with in handling their own feelings. So, school could be the answer. One of the staff there — pick the teacher you like best — should be able to help you talk. Or, if you belong to a Church, talking to the minister may be the answer. But basically, death is a fact of life all of us have to learn to live with, somehow. It isn't easy. I'm still learning.

Question 3 "*My father and mother have been separated eight years. Last year I started to see my mother again without my dad knowing. He disagrees with me seeing her because he thinks my recent step-mother is good enough. How can I get round to telling him that I still love my own mother and that I am seeing her? I'm fifteen.*"

Answer It's hell to be in your situation. It's like being the rope in a tug of war. I happen to think your father is foolish to feel that your normal desire to keep in touch with your natural mother is disloyalty to his new wife, but if that's the way he reacts there's little you can do to alter it. So although I usually believe that talking honestly to people is the best way to resolve strife, in your case I'm going to say that discretion is the answer, at least for the time being. In other words, see your mother quietly when you have the chance, talk to her on the phone when you can, and say nothing to your dad. In time, as you get older, you'll develop the maturity that will enable you to tell him without hurting him that you've maintained your contacts with your mum. And maybe by then he'll be more relaxed and will see how unreasonable he's been. Part of being a successful young person, remember,

136 Growing Pains

is understanding the difficulties experienced by older people. It isn't *always* the other way around.

Question 4 "*I'm 16 and still suck my thumb. I have tried to get out of the 'baby' habit but I just can't. I am so embarrassed about my problem.*"

Answer If you really can't stop the habit of your own free will, then please, *stop trying*. Accept it as one of those things that is part of you, and shrug your shoulders. It's the only remedy, because this is a comfort habit, and the more you worry about it, the more comforting you need, and the more you feel driven to it. Your actual vicious circle. And it isn't all that terrible a habit, after all. Personally, I'd rather see a person with his or her thumb in his mouth than a lethal cigarette. Smoking is of course first cousin to thumb sucking and nail biting. Once you stop trying to stop, by the way, it's very likely it will stop by itself.

Question 5 "*I've had a Saturday job for over a year. I don't get a lot for it, but I like it — it's in a pet shop — and the money comes in handy. Now my dad was made redundant and money is short at home, so I wanted to help out and said I'd give him half my Saturday money. He went mad and told me I was getting at him, but I wasn't really and now I feel so bad. I want to give up the job because of it all but my mum says I shouldn't, and she said I can give her half the money, and Dad needn't know. But that makes it more difficult, because he'll think I don't care, won't he?*"

Answer It's sad when a genuinely meant generous action is misunderstood — and that is all that happened between you and your dad of course. It could be you jumped in too soon with your kind offer before he had had a chance to regain his balance after the shock of his redundancy. It can shatter a man who has always managed to maintain his family well when he loses his job; it's not just loss of money but loss of status, of control, of authority, of self-esteem that hurts. And having you, the young male who will of course one day be more dominant than he is himself, seeking to jump at once on his losses made it feel much worse. He didn't see your offer as generous but as a sort of triumphant whoop. Of course that hurts your feelings, but when people are suffering pain themselves they sadly often inflict it on others — even those they love. Try to understand and forgive him — and for heaven's sake tell your mum that this must be sorted out properly. To let you contribute to the household while not telling your dad is to *increase* his sense of failure when the time comes and he discovers the truth, as of course he will. I think you must ask her to be honest with him if she is to go on taking your money. Or, if she can't, to stop taking it, because doing so puts you in an impossible position, doesn't it? It makes you feel deceitful, and that's a horrible way to feel. One thing is sure — don't give up your job. You won't give your father a thing by depriving yourself of your job. You'll only chip away even more at his sense of self worth.

Question 6 *"Please help. My mum drinks a lot. I'm an only child of 15 and the only person who knows, because I get home from school and she's asleep on the kitchen table and I can smell it on her. By the time Dad gets home at seven she's woken up and cleaned up a bit and seems O.K., though I can't understand why he doesn't notice how awful she looks these days and how nasty tempered she is. I can't tell him because he gets mad if I don't mind my own business about things, and I can't tell her, can I? But I'm so scared. She could set fire to herself or something one day, couldn't she?"*

Answer It's my guess your dad does know something is wrong but chooses not to face up to it. That does happen, I'm afraid, in families where alcoholism happens. And you certainly can't cope with this situation unaided. You've got to get help, and it won't be disloyal to tell someone else what is happening in your home. Have you grandparents? Aunts, uncles, trusted family friends? If not, then it has to be a teacher at school you can trust, someone who will talk to your dad, and see to it that he arranges for her to get the medical care she needs. Don't forget the family doctor, too. He's someone else who may be able to help. You can ask him to call at the house one afternoon at the time you know your mum is drunk — tell him what you fear is happening and he should take over. You can get personal help on coming to terms with what's happening by contacting Alateen, the organisation that was set up for teenagers in families where there is a drink problem. [The address is in the Information Section at the end of the book.]

CHAPTER EIGHT
YOU AND YOUR LOVE LIFE

If you ask most people in their teens which aspect of their lives causes them most concern, you'd probably be told, "Love". Or, if the people you asked were really honest, "Sex". And though sex and love are by no means the same thing, the two are curled up together in a very tight tangle indeed so both answers would be honest.

Lots of people get anxious about their own sexual feelings long before they start to think about sexual patterns. In Chapter I I've considered one of them — anxiety about masturbation. It's nothing to be anxious about is the basic message because it's normal and indeed a most useful and enjoyable part of sexual development.

Some people told that will still worry because of the thoughts they have while they are masturbating — their fantasy life. Well stop worrying — fantasies of this kind are perfectly normal.

Nature, the basic life force, is interested in only one thing — survival of the species, be it hornets or horses or humans. One of the ways she encourages us all to reproduce ourselves, and so keep the species going, is to make copulation deeply pleasurable. And because it is so pleasurable, inevitably we, the thinking animals, think about the pleasure often. Fantasies and all.

The interesting thing about sexy thoughts is that they are both caused *by* hormone activity (the body's chemical messenger system which controls such activities as metabolism, growth and reproduction) and directly cause it. In other words, when a person's body is hormonally needing sex, the mind fills with sexy thoughts, and when the mind fills with sexy thoughts, the body's hormone balance changes, and make it ready for sex. It's a feedback loop, in the scientific jargon.

This explains why it is that a person who sees a sexually stimulating sight, be it a potential real live partner or a picture in a magazine or a scene in a film, gets physical reactions. A boy may get an erection — his penis prepares itself for sex by filling up with blood which makes it stiff and upright so that it stands away from the body at an angle — just the right firmness and shape to enter a vagina, and a girl finds her vulva becomes warmer, swells a little and she produces slippery liquid which may escape from her vagina as a clear discharge. Just right to accept an erect penis comfortably.

When this happens the need to relieve the build up of sexual drive can be powerful, and if there's no partner around to help you do that, then self-help is the obvious answer. And to keep the feedback loop working and the hormones busy, continued thinking about sexiness is needed. Which is why people usually fantasise while they masturbate.

It is a normal and natural thing.

And that is true whatever your fantasy happens to be. There are people who imagine ordinary straightforward intercourse with a specific person. There are people who imagine intercourse with a stranger. Some who imagine it with an exotic stranger — a robber baron or a deep sea diver or whatever it is that they happen to find interesting at that time. In the 1920s lots of girls fantasised about sex with Arabs in flowing robes, all because of an actor called Rudolph Valentino who was very beautiful and sexy to look at, and who played the lead in a hugely successful film called *The Sheik*.

There are also people who imagine sex with lots of partners — the harem sort of fantasy — and both sexes share this one. Or sex which involves force — being overwhelmed by a person stronger and more knowledgeable than you are — and again, both sexes have this sort. In fact I could go on listing different fantasies for the rest of this book in order to reassure readers that their particular fantasy is one they share with hordes of others, but that would get boring.

So that is one anxiety you can set aside, if you have it. Whatever you fantasise, you can be sure that millions have had the same fantasy before you — and millions yet unborn will have it when they reach adult life.

What is real sex like?

One of the problems with young sexual fantasy is that it has to be based, very often, on inadequate knowledge. School sex education may provide a great deal of the sort of nuts and bolts information that I gave in Chapter I — and it's very necessary information — but beyond explaining that a penis has to be inserted into a vagina and sperm released in order to make a conception happen, school sex education, by and large, offers little about what sex really feels like.

For a very good reason: it's a very hard thing to explain. Each individual responds differently. There are of course basic patterns into which we all fit roughly, but individual experience is very much that — *individual*. So telling young people in great detail that when they have intercourse this will happen first and then that will happen next and the other will happen finally can upset them when they come to try sex for themselves because they discover, to their consternation, that it isn't quite like that. It will be a totally personal experience.

But having said that, I'm still prepared to have a go and try to describe what sexual experience is like. But *please* do remember that there is no universal law to govern all that I'll describe. It may be like this for you — and it may not.

Sexual attraction

Why one person is attracted to another tends to be a mystery. It isn't just looks that matter — because looks are a matter of fashion as much as clothes. In one era girls with big busts and bottoms will be "fashionable" and boys with broad shoulders and strong muscles will be "in" and, lo and behold, all the people who look like that are beseiged by would-be sexual partners. But a couple of generations later a female beauty may be considered to be thin, almost breastless and with a narrow bottom, while the "ideal" handsome man is also skinny to the point of emaciation with hardly any shoulders at all. And *they* are the ones everyone pants after. Yet all the "unfashionable" looking people find themselves partners in due course if they want them (not everyone does, by the way — there are lots of people who can live very contentedly without sex at all) so fashionable looks aren't really all that important.

One thing is sure — there is no special chemistry that links two people as inevitably as one piece of jigsaw fits another. In fact, there is no such thing as sexual compatability — any girl and any boy can build a very satisfactory sex relationship, if they want to. That has to be obvious — if we all really were jigsaw puzzle pieces hunting the world for each other, most of us would end our lives alone and unloved and unsatisfied. The odds against meeting our Perfect Partner would be too great.

Sometimes people fancy each other because they are themselves ready for sexuality. Your own stage of maturity has a lot to do with the way you feel about other people. If you are ripe for love, and happen across someone else in the same state, wham!, magic happens.

Sometimes it happens because the love object bears a strong resemblance to someone you already love. If you're the daughter of a smashing affectionate father or the son of a delightful and loving mother, the day you meet someone who looks or sounds vaguely like that parent you'll be halfway to falling in love with them. There's a comfortable familiarity about their appearance, and what seems to be a built-in reassurance that they are lovable. In fact the resemblance may be only skin deep — that smashing boy who looks so like your loving dad may turn out to be a selfish manipulator or whinger — the very opposite of what you expected. That's why some people fall out of love as fast as they fall in.

And some people fall in love with people who look rather like themselves. The familiarity of a face they see in their own mirror every day makes it seem very attractive

Whatever the reason for sexual attraction, it's there. And it does some interesting things to you when you first talk to the person to whom you are attracted.

These are interesting because, as you will have noticed, some of them are exactly the same as those you get when you're shy (see Chapter 7). They are part of the same response — a surge of adrenalin — though this surge is due not to the sight of a runaway lorry, but the sight of a sexually interesting person. There are two listed here, however, that I didn't comment on before, even though they do happen in a fight/flight situation too, because they are particularly interesting in sexual excitement.

They are *enlarged eye pupils*, and *subliminal smell changes*.

The *eye changes* happen when the pupil widens to admit more light — in effect, to increase the amount that is seen. A person facing a threat needs to see more, to enable him to evaluate the degree of a threat — and a person gripped by sexual interest wants to be able to see as much of what is sexually interesting as possible.

This enlargement and therefore darkening of the eye is so much a part of sexual arousal that it acts as a sexual trigger in itself and forms a feedback loop. That is, A sees B and finds B a sexy sight, so his eyes darken as the pupils enlarge. B might not have noticed A until then — but the sight of those dark eyes triggers matching feelings in her. Her attraction to him makes her eyes darken and there they are — attracting each other like mad. All very convenient.

Nowadays we have such aids as eyeshadow and mascara to make our eyes look extra sexy. (Well, women do, at any rate. It's tough on the men — they have to actually feel sexy to get the effect.)

The *smell changes* are interesting because you can't yourself actually smell them — or you don't think you do. But they get to your nose and

Subliminal changes in body odour
Enlarged pupils to the eyes
Tightness in the belly
Sweating of hands, face and body
breathlessness
Flushing, then pallor
increased heart beat
maybe some hand trembling
Jelly knees

Boy meets Girl

thence to your brain, even if you're not aware of the fact. That is why they're called *subliminal* — they're below the level of your awareness.

These smells are due to substances called *pheremones* which are a little like out-of-the-body hormones, in that they can act on the recipient's hormones. A sees B and fancies her, and starts to sweat more because he is aroused. The sweat contains sexual pheremones which reach her nose (they can travel across a very wide space) and enter her brain, trigger her hormones and make her aware of that sexy man across the room. She doesn't know she smells him — but she does. Her hormones, stirred by his pheremones, swing into action. She gets aroused, sweats a little, makes her own pheremones which reach him — and again, we're off. A pair of people getting a great charge from each other.

It's neat, isn't it? Nature is nothing if not resourceful.

People are resourceful too, of course. Lots of us use perfumes which contain very similar smells to natural sexy ones, as part of our sexual attraction system. Often it's money wasted; a clean healthy body can smell much more exciting than an artificially scented one — because it smells genuinely sexy.

Incidentally, these pheremones aren't only nice sexy attractive ones. There are others — like those produced by frightened people. They signal fear to bystanders, and make them fearful in their turn. Which is

144 *Growing Pains*

why one frightened person in a crowd can actually trigger a wave of panic. There are also aggression-stirring pheremones — which is why one tough in a football crowd can be at the core of a wave of rowdyism.

We now have a situation in which two people fancy each other. What happens next?

There is a progression through which a couple pass.

As you can see, there are six stages between first meeting and attraction to full intercourse.

STAGE ONE which is meeting and talking can go on for a very long time. There are people, particularly shy or unself-confident ones, who can prolong it for many months. Or, it may be that one person is more attracted than the other, and they have to spend a good deal of time meeting, talking, getting to know each other before they reach a matching state of sexual interest. This is what "courting" is all about.

This is a great stage, and can be a lot of fun, full of surprises and hope and excitement. It can also be a very distressing stage, if the beloved object doesn't respond as much as the in-love person would like. There can be lots of yearning and crying, lots of doubts and jealousy and anger.

If you're unlucky, stage one may be the end of the road. You may never get beyond it with this particular partner. But be assured, you will with the next. Or the next —

STAGE TWO is more intimate. You've both admitted, if not in so many words, that you both like each other. You go out together, sit close together when you have the chance, touch each other as much as possible without being obviously sexy.

This touching and togetherness is intensely exciting, giving the adrenalin surge another shove and increasing the trembling/sweating/breathlessness state more and more. It's all very agreeable.

This stage tends to be shorter than stage one. When a couple reach it they are ready for a faster rate of travel. (In fact some people skip it altogether.) However, it may be prolonged by factors outside your control. Being very young — under fourteen or so — may mean you are extra protected by your parents, and have little chance to get together for the next stages. Or you may live among people where it is considered wrong for young people to be together in private — this is the way life is run in some Asian cultures — and so chaperonage keeps you stuck at this stage. In the past, of course, young people who lived in "respectable" middle-class households had very little opportunity to get past stage two — until they were engaged, and so pushed on the road to the final stage.

STAGE THREE is another short one and may blur into stage two — cuddling. The hand touching and arm brushing become more deliberate. You walk along with arms round each other. You whisper in each other's ears, cheek to cheek. You dance closely. Etcetera.

STAGE FOUR is a major step forwards — the beginning of real kissing. There may have been some light kissing in stage three — cheek kissing — but now it's a matter of lips to lips. And eventually the so-called "French kiss" or "deep kiss". In this each person open his/her mouth, and admits the tongue of the other, and also puts his/her own tongue in the other's mouth.

If a couple are really ready for this degree of intimacy — and deep kissing is very intimate indeed — then it's very exciting and gives the adrenalin surge a tremendous kick upwards. BUT — and this is very important — if one of the participants really isn't ready for that degree of closeness, the effect can be not excitement but revulsion. And many are the hopeful love affairs that have been ruined because one or other was in too much of a hurry with a tongue. The unready one runs off the road altogether.

But if both partners *are* ready, during deep kissing a number of sexual reactions happen. They can also happen even at the second stage (remember, every person is different!) and the most obvious one in a boy is a firm erection. In a girl, it is the production of lubricating liquid in the vagina, together with some swelling of the vulva, accompanied by throbbing and pleasant sensations focussed on the *clitoris*. In addition, a girl may feel her breasts tighten and ache slightly as her nipples harden and become erect. *It doesn't happen to all girls.* Just some.

STAGE FIVE which is the *petting* stage may follow rapidly on stage four, or there may be a long period during which the couple stay in stage four. It depends on many factors — age for example (very young lovers are sometimes unready to go much further than close kissing) or depth of sexual knowledge (people who know little about sex may be scared to go beyond kissing — which is all right while you're still very young, say in mid-teens, but rather sad if you're an adult, say in mid-twenties).

There is also a very simple practical aspect — the availability of privacy, because petting is a much more intimate stage which demands time and aloneness.

Petting means caressing each other. In *light petting* it consists mainly of stroking of each other's clothed bodies — a boy will put his hands over his girl's breasts, but not attempt to unbutton her shirt or touch skin and often won't try to touch her below the waist. A girl will stroke his back and thighs, and may put her hand over his clothed genitals — though not always — but won't try, again, to touch skin.

In a few cases, some people become so aroused that they experience the peak of sexual excitement. An orgasm, or *climax*. This is an uprush of sensation which in a boy is accompanied by the emission of semen, sperm in liquid, which comes out of the penis in little spurts. In a girl, there is a similar feeling accompanied by rhythmic tightening and then relaxing on the walls of the vagina but no emission. Both feel hot, breathless, have a rapid heartbeat, and very much enjoy the feeling. Both afterwards feel relaxed, sleepy and not very sexy any more. In some people, there may be such a change of feeling, compared with the pre-climax excitement, that they feel depressed, even tearful.

All this varies enormously from one person to another — and it is by no means an inevitable part of this stage. It just happens *to some*.

STAGE SIX is a natural development of stage five and is often called *heavy petting*. In this, the couple caress each other's bare skin, using their hands, and also kiss each other's bodies (including sex organs). Boys will kiss the girl's nipples, may suckle at them the way a baby does, and both may give each other "lovebites". These are small red

You and Your Love Life   147

marks which appear when a small area of skin is pulled into the mouth and sucked in, hard. It causes little blood vessels to break down and bleed into the skin tissues. They are harmless, comparatively painless, do not cause nasty diseases like cancer, though they can cause a lot of comment if they appear in obvious places, like the neck, which is a very easy site to lovebite, because the skin there is so flexible.

Couples vary in the way they caress and stimulate each other during heavy petting, and really loving couples talk about the way they are making love so that they can provide their partner with the most enjoyable caresses. No one is born knowing how to make love; it is a skill that has to be learned. And showing and talking with someone you love is the best way to learn.

The completion of heavy petting is deliberate creation of an orgasm. A boy can help his girl to reach her climax by gently rubbing the clitoris — (this is sometimes called "fingering") and a girl can bring a boy to his by rubbing his penis with her fist half closed (this is sometimes called "wanking off").

Once again each couple will share different patterns of lovemaking which suit them. *There are no rules.*

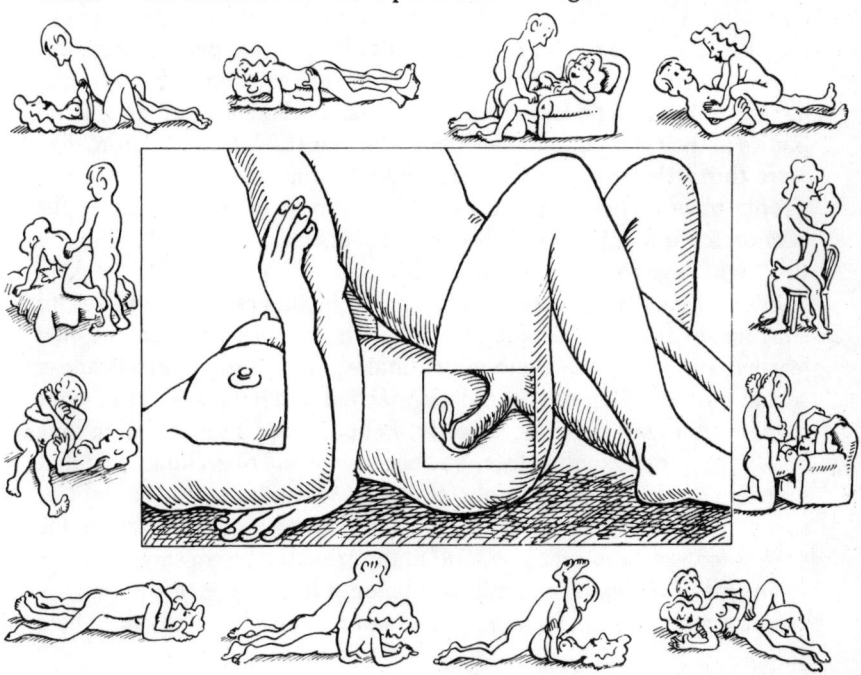

The final stage is of course complete intercourse. In the past no one really knew for sure what actually happened in the body during intercourse — no one had ever seen a penis inside a vagina — but American researchers called Masters and Johnson wired people up with lights and electric devices so they could actually measure what happened.

So much then, for the nuts and bolts of sexual activity — but please don't think that I have in these past few pages described love. I haven't because I can't. No one can. Poets and painters and musicians have for centuries been trying to convey what sexual love feels like and have never yet really succeeded. It is something you have to experience for yourself. But it will help, when the time comes, to have some knowledge of the physical aspects of lovemaking. And now you have that.

When the time comes. That is a key question for many young people. When *has* the time come to start a sex life?

Am I ready for sex?

People have agonised about this question over the centuries more than about important ones like how can people learn to stop making war on each other, and how can we learn to share out the world's good things more fairly, and still haven't found an answer.

It's no use saying, "When they are sexually mature," because some girls start their periods before they leave their primary school aged eleven, and some boys reach the stage of having frequent emissions of semen as young as twelve or so. And it's obvious that people of this age in our society couldn't cope with the pressures of an adult sex life. Children living in primitive societies possibly did start having sex and babies in their late childhood — but when most adults died before they were thirty that made biological sense. In our complex world where people have to learn and work and take part of the burden of the economics of life, it doesn't. So, physical development is no pointer to the "right" age for starting a sex life.

In the nineteenth century, and earlier in this century, the key to starting sex for most people was *economic* maturity. When you had learned enough to earn enough to make a living for yourself and a sexual partner — that is, could get married and have a home of your own — you were considered ready. People could and did fall in love and want to be sexually close, but because of the prevailing view that marriage, a proper legal public contract, was the key to the door of sexual fulfillment, the majority tried not to go beyond stage five on the road to complete intercourse, and many tried to stay in stage four.

The idea that sexual commitment belongs to a marriage and that sex before a marriage can be damaging is not necessarily a bad one. There was and still is some good hard commonsense underlying this point of view.

Rushing into sex can spoil it. People who pooh-pooh the idea that marriage and commitment matter tend to streak along the road so fast that they go virtually from stage one to full intercourse in one bound, bypassing the intermediate stages altogether.

And that's self-defeating. Sex, to be really all it can be, needs time. Sex shared with someone you hardly know, and with whom you have not passed through the intermediate stages, is never as satisfying as sex shared with someone you know well and like as well as fancy. If you add love to the mix then you really have the ingredients for satisfying sex.

Too many young people have been bitterly disappointed in their first sexual experience because they haven't realised this, and tried it with the first person of the right gender who happened along. I know. I deal with their letters of misery and confusion and regret.

A good marriage has a better chance of offering the ingredients for good sex if a couple are marrying for the right reason; the right reason being a genuine love for each other which has been tested over several months — a year or more if possible — and which is underpinned by practical efforts to build a home to be shared.

Some people marry for the wrong reasons, of course — like to be fashionable (all their friends are getting married) or to get away from Mum and Dad (not everyone enjoys living at home) or to be in charge of their own lives (getting married sounds such a mature thing to do that some people think that just doing it makes them mature, though of course it doesn't; it just underlines the degree of their immaturity) or because they whizzed too fast down the road to intercourse and got pregnant (making a baby together doesn't mean you've made a good relationship together) or because they simply haven't thought enough about what it is they're really doing. For them marriage does *not* promise good sex.

But get the marriage right, and the sex will usually work out right too. *Eventually*. Because a good sexual relationship takes time to grow. Two people, however much in love they are, have to learn together to give and take sexual love — and a sound young marriage gives them space in which to do that.

So don't throw your hands up in disgust at elders who go on about the importance of marriage. They aren't just being conventional or narrow-minded. They're trying to tell you, if not as clearly as might be, that marriage is more likely to provide a safe framework within which you can enjoy sex.

Incidentally in using the word marriage today, many people — me included — are referring not only to couples who have gone through a religious/legal process, but also those who choose to live together as a committed pair. A marriage means commitment, whether endorsed ceremoniously or not.

But all this still doesn't give an answer to the question: "When are people ready for sex?"

There's another sort of maturity, and that's the one that is the key. *Emotional maturity.*

AN EMOTIONALLY MATURE PERSON is one who understands some of the bases of his own feelings (no one can understand them all!) and cope with the more disagreeable ones.

AN EMOTIONALLY MATURE PERSON has self-esteem but also concern for others.

AN EMOTIONALLY MATURE PERSON can wait to gratify his own needs — he doesn't insist that he's got to have what he wants the minute he wants it.

AN EMOTIONALLY MATURE PERSON is kind to himself — he does not expect himself always to be perfect in every way.

AN EMOTIONALLY MATURE PERSON is kind to others in the same way — he makes allowances for their shortcomings and less attractive aspects.

AN EMOTIONALLY MATURE PERSON thinks for himself — he doesn't let other people tell him how to feel.

There are other factors which go into the mix which is emotional maturity. I'm still trying to find out what all of them are myself, because no one ever attains complete maturity. Which is why I haven't got all the answers yet.

But you can tell if you are a mature person by the way you face up to things: you can handle disappointment, you can delay immediate gratification in order to enjoy future benefits, you are willing to see your own faults, and give other people respect and space in which to be themselves. And if you meet a person who is as emotionally mature as you are, then it is possible that you can build a relationship that will lead to a mutual readiness for sex that will give both of you pleasure and neither of you distress.

Which doesn't mean that, armed with this information, you should rush off to find a sexual partner straight away. That would be very immature!

Is it love?

But knowing whether or not you are emotionally mature isn't the only factor you need for a sexual relationship. You need to be really in love — and that means a very different thing to being merely infatuated. How can you tell the difference between the two? Well, here are some guidelines:

You can't be in love with someone you don't know — like an actor or pop star. Real love demands above all real knowledge of a person.

You can't be in love with someone's lifestyle — snappy dresser, smart car, glamorous job, or the reverse of all of those. It's the person behind the façade that counts.

You can't be in love with someone just because your parents think he/she is terrific, or because they think he/she is awful. It's what *you* think that matters.

You can't be in love with someone if you only use them to show off to your friends.

You can't be in love with someone if you flirt with other people.

You can't be in love with someone if you always have to put on a show in front of them and hide your natural self.

You can't be in love with someone if you're not prepared to accept them at their worst — like when they are ill or miserable.

You can't be in love with someone unless you're prepared to share everything with them.

If you examine your innermost feelings, you'll know if it's the real thing.

How far should I go?

This is another question many people ask. They feel sexually mature. They believe themselves to be in love. But they know they are too young for a committed and long-term relationship, though they need some expression of their sexual feelings.

Oh, but this is a tough one to answer! There is one school of thought that says, "Young people should do no more than a little hand holding and simple kissing and cuddling". And another that says, "Young people are at the peak of their sexual drive and it's impossible to stop them having complete sex. As long as they make sure they don't start a pregnancy, then they should go ahead."

I belong to neither school of thought. I don't think you can make hard and fast rules for other people on how they lead their lives. So, to answer the question, "How far should I go?" I'm going to answer with another question. "How far do *you* think you should go?" If you feel too confused to answer it, then the wise thing to do is *as little as possible* — because what is done can't be undone. If you're not sure whether you want to go all the way to complete intercourse, and while you're still trying to decide go ahead anyway, then you're cheating on yourself, aren't you? You must *think* first, act afterwards.

It may help you to think more constructively if you and your partner talk a lot about your ideas on the subject. The more you discuss, the more you'll understand your own needs and moral attitudes and religious beliefs, and each other's. A girl may find, after talking, that in fact she isn't ready for more than stage two or three lovemaking — but that she's being pushed by her boyfriend. I hate to sound sexist, but the facts are facts here: by and large, boys are more urgent in their desire for complete sex, more likely than girls to put on pressure, more likely to try subtle — or even outright — sexual and emotional blackmail. ("If you really loved me you would — "; "What's the matter with you — are you frigid or something?"; "Well, if you won't, someone else will"; "Are you a lesbian?" and so on.) Not all boys of course do this; many are sensitive, thoughtful, genuinely able to put their girl's feelings before their own. But many more are not. So a girl needs to be sure of what sort of boy she's dealing with when she talks to him. And of course, boys too need to realise that there are some girls who push them for sex before they are really ready for it — some girls reach their maturity so far in advance of boys that their sexual needs are greater. Talking it out helps both partners to estimate the situation.

And, if you can, talk to your parents, your teachers, other adults you know and trust. If you can't find such an adult in your immediate environment, look at the back of the book for information about other sources of guidance.

If you do decide that you are ready to go all the way to complete intercourse, then you need to know about contraception. Indeed, you need to know about it whether or not you're ready to use it yet. This sort of practical information is essential equipment for any young adult.

You will need contraception, by the way, not only if you are going to have complete sex, but also if you are petting to climax — stage five. Once a boy's semen is ejaculated, the sperms are available to fertilise an egg cell. And if they are ejaculated near a girl's vulva, or even reach it from a boy's fingers, if she is at a particularly fertile stage (at ovulation time) it is just possible for a conception to happen. It's rare — but it's not impossible. So, a boy could use a sheath if he's petting to climax, to be on the safe side, and a girl could use a chemical as well. (See chart on pages 154—5.)

What about abortion?

Some people are offhand about using contraception, telling themselves they can "always get an abortion".

More hard facts are needed here. First, it isn't as easy as some people think to arrange an abortion. A girl can't just walk into a hospital and say casually, "Get rid of this pregnancy for me", and have it done. Doctors have to be consulted, and careful discussion entered into before it is agreed to operate. Also, in some areas of the country availability of National Health abortions is very limited, and people may need money to get the help they need (though the abortion charities do their best to help everyone, whether they can pay or not).

And, even more importantly, it is an emotionally painful experience. Until you've been pregnant, you can't know what it feels like — but many girls who have thought they could cheerfully get rid of an unwanted conception find they mourn bitterly the loss of their baby. We are driven by a deeper biological and psychological need than many of us realise. So the result of an abortion can be for some girls depression and misery and spoiled relationships — and often another pregnancy almost at once, because these girls are driven by their feelings to replace the baby they thought they wanted to get rid of.

This is why contraception is important. To lock the stable door makes sense. To damage the horse, lassoing it after it's got out, does not.

If a girl has conceived and wants help to sort out what to do, she can get advice from a number of sources (see Information Section at the back of the book). If she is in any doubt at all about what she wants to do, she should avoid the organisations which are known to be either pro-abortion or anti-abortion. Their counsellors, even though they may not realise they are doing it, may put on subtle pressures to persuade a girl to do what they think she should do, rather than letting her decide for herself. If in doubt, go to your local social services department and ask to talk to a social worker. These are people trained

CONTRACEPTION FACTS

METHOD	HOW DOES IT WORK?	HOW EFFECTIVE IS IT?	PROBLEMS	WHERE TO GET IT
ABSTENTION	No sex at all	100%	Frustration	—
PILL (tablets containing hormones) taken by mouth by girl.	Prevents egg cell from being produced: no egg, no pregnancy.	If used *absolutely* according to instructions 99.9%	Not suitable for girls with existing hormone disorders. Also some girls have side-effects; headaches; weight gain; breast tenderness, etc.	G.P. Family planning clinic Youth advisory centre.
BARRIER METHODS				
A) SHEATH (condom, French letter, Durex, rubber, Johnny).	Rubber cover over penis catches sperms, preventing them getting into girl's body.	If used carefully, together with chemical 92.5%	Can only be put on erect penis, so interrupts lovemaking. Dulls sensation for a boy in some cases.	Family planning clinic, chemists, barber shops, slot machines.
B) CAP	A rubber barrier is put over the cervix (neck of the uterus).	If properly fitted and if used with a chemical 92.8%	Some girls dislike having to handle their own bodies when putting the cap in.	G.P. Family planning clinic Youth advisory centre.
CHEMICALS				
A) Aerosol foams, e.g. Delfen, Emko.	Foam put into vagina makes a thick chemical barrier sperms can't cross, so sperms are immobilised or killed before they can enter uterus. Jellies and tablets have similar effect.	Almost as effective as caps/sheaths 90.8%	Some girls are sensitive to chemicals. Others find them messy. Must always be used *immediately* before sex.	Chemist (no prescription)
B) Creams, jellies, pastes, soluble tablets e.g. Orthocream, Stacept, Rendells, Duracream.		Not very reliable used alone; used with caps/sheaths 92.8%		

I.U.D. (Intra-uterine contraceptive device.) Coil; loop; spiral; safe T; Copper 7 (Gravigard); etc.	Small piece of plastic (sometimes containing copper) is put inside uterus. It seems to prevent fertilised cells from implanting to become a baby.	If no problems (see next column) 97.5%	Not suitable for girls who have not had babies. Some women "push" the device out; others suffer cramps, heavy periods. Also may lead to infection in some cases.	G.P. Family planning clinic
"SAFE" PERIOD (Rhythm)	Date of ovulation (egg production) is worked out by taking temperature every day or using calendar. Then sex is avoided during fertile days.	If sex is restricted to days *after* ovulation, only then 94%. If *not* 82%.	Demands considerable self-control from both partners and awareness that no girl's cycle is really reliable.	Thermometer, charts from chemist.
WITHDRAWAL ("Being careful") Coitus interruptus	Boy withdraws his penis from vagina just when he feels orgasm about to happen.	Difficult to assess. Apparently used quite widely all over world. But probably very unreliable.	May fail, since boy may withdraw too late, or some sperm may leave his penis before orgasm. Some girls find it unsatisfactory and frustrating.	—
"HOLDING BACK" (girl prevents herself from reaching climax).	It doesn't. Even without orgasm a pregnancy can happen.	Not at all.	Frustration as well as risky.	—

not to take sides. Of course, they're people too and have their own views on abortion, and so may also be at risk of putting on pressure — but you've a good chance of getting the right support from them.

And remember too that parents and boyfriends may try to put pressure on a pregnant girl, either to abort or keep the baby. By all means listen to them — they are involved in your decision, after all — but listen to the social worker as well. He or she will have less emotional involvement in your pregnancy, and so can help you best.

What sort of sex do I want?

So far, we've looked at sex as though it were always a matter of boy/girl relationships. But it isn't. There is a large number of people who find their sex in boy/boy or girl/girl relationships, all their adult lives.

And there are a large number of people who find their sex in boy/boy or girl/girl relationships at different stages of their lives.

The label used for same-gender sexual relationships is homosexuality. Unhappily this has come to be an almost dirty word in some people's ears — *but I do not regard homosexuality as a "perversion" or "dirty" or "sinful" or "queer" or "bent" or any other label of that sort.*

I see it as an aspect of human loving that is no less valuable nor more valuable than any other. It just *is* — a part of the person who happens to feel it at that time. (And, incidentally, this is an opinion shared by a great many informed and thoughtful people.)

Many young people get very agitated if they find they have homosexual feelings, mostly because they have been brought up by adults who share the Bible's rejection of homosexual love (and even the non-religious often think like the old Bible people) and may even panic, thinking themselves uniquely damaged in some way, or uniquely wicked.

They are not. Most young people, left to themselves, will move from same-sex to opposite-sex relationships and back again as they pass through their process of finding their emotional maturity. It's all part of learning to love and feel. And if you are one of the people — estimated to be 10 per cent, but probably more — who is destined to spend your life relating mostly to your own sex, that doesn't mean that you're peculiar. You may be in the minority, but it's a very large minority. The present world population is said to be four billion, and that means if there are just 10 per cent who are homosexual there are four hundred million. You're among friends, aren't you?

Actually that isn't quite the way to put it, because of course people are much more different in their ways and attitudes and responses than just in their sexual responses. Not all people who are homosexual will like each other and feel friendly with each other, any more than all heterosexuals do.

Unfortunately, a great many uninformed people do have the idea that all homosexual people are the same. They have a stereotype of the male homosexual that says he is limp-wristed, talks in a silly sort of sing-song voice, is interested only in ballet dancing and interior design, and spends as much time as possible trying to seduce little boys. There is a matching stereotype for girls who are homosexual (lesbian is another word). They are supposed to be large, loud-voiced, cigar-smoking short-haired bullies who wear collars and ties whenever they can.

Daft, isn't it?

The facts are that among men there are beer-swilling rugger-playing six-foot-three hearties who are homosexual, and delicate dreamy-eyed ballet dancers who are heterosexual.

There are among women tall and pushy engineers who are heterosexual, and sweet submissive frilly housewives who are homosexual.

There are no stereotypes — unless people want to be one.

Some people wonder why homosexual feelings arise, when the "natural" reason for sex is reproduction. It must be a sign of something wrong in the individual's system when biological laws are flouted this way, they say.

Well, if we were just reproducing machines that might be true. If humans only ever engaged in sex to make a new human being, then fair enough. But we don't operate that way. It's because we have our big brains and the vivid imagination that comes from them, and the desire for interest and stimulation all the time, that we have turned sex into more than just a method of baby-making. For us it's the great game. We play it for all sorts of reasons — for fun, for the giving and taking of love, for comfort — the list is enormous. And playing a game with the same sex is as reasonable and natural as playing it with the opposite one.

Another reason for young people experiencing homosexual feelings is "modelling". Growing up is difficult — and just as when you're doing a jigsaw puzzle it helps to have a picture on the lid of the box to follow, so it helps when you're growing up to have another person to copy — model on. So, lots of young people find they develop a crush on someone of their own sex as well as getting sexy feelings towards members of the opposite sex. They're really saying, "I want to be like that person". And in time, as the individual gets to be more sure of the new adult he or she is becoming, the crush wears away, as the need for an image wears away. When you've finished the jigsaw puzzle you don't need the picture any more.

By the way, something of the same sort is happening when people get a crush on someone of the opposite sex whom they don't know — a pop star, or an actress. As part of the growth towards sexual maturity a person has to learn to feel, "This is the sort of lover I want" — and rehearses the way he or she *will* feel when the real person turns up, by "falling in love" with an image. Of course people like Sting of the Police and Debbie Harry are real — but unless you actually know them personally, they're as unreal as Father Christmas and the Christmas tree fairy. Creatures to yearn after but not to have.

Never panic if you get these feelings. They're normal, they're interesting — if sometimes painful — and your life would be much more tragic if you were incapable of having such feelings at all.

Teacher/boss crushes

Some people get crushes on their teachers (or their bosses), of the same or opposite sex, and these of course are more difficult-to-handle feelings in that they are aimed at a real person you actually know, rather than at an image. Often the root of the feelings is again modelling; or it may be due to the need all young people have to grow out of their dependence on Mum and Dad, the hitherto most important adults in their lives, so that they're free to love others. And a teacher especially, who is a sort of parent, even if young and quite glamorous, makes a handy "bridge" person to love until you're ready to love a really equal partner.

BUT BE WARNED. Unless you want to create all sorts of anguish and misery for yourself as well as for the teacher on whom you have a crush, you will *never* make any attempt to get closer to the teacher than is normal classroom contact. Most teachers have an understanding of crushes; they understand the need to avoid hurt feelings and risky situations by keeping a distance between themselves and pupils. But a few may be vulnerable and silly, and there is nothing more damaging for either teacher or pupil than headlines about scandals involving "school sweetheart runaways", and all the rest of it. Teachers are teachers, not potential love partners either hetero- or homo-sexual. Never forget that.

Who may I love?

People don't worry only about the gender of those with whom they fall in love — they also worry about the relationship that may exist between them.

For example, it is not at all uncommon for cousins to fall in love. It's natural enough; they share some common family experience, have probably known each other most of their lives, and there may be a family resemblance which makes them more attractive to each other.

There is no need to be upset if this happens to you.

Under British law, sexual relationships between cousins (including first cousins) are perfectly legal, though some religious groups may disapprove. If a pair of cousins decide to marry however, it is well worth their while discussing their family medical history with a Genetic Counselling Unit, which can make an informed estimate of any risk of passing on a family disorder to children. This can be arranged via the GP.

But there are other family relationships which cannot become sexual relationships, and which are not permissible. As everyone knows, fathers and daughters, mothers and sons and brothers and sisters may not legally share sexual contact. This is not to say that it never happens; there are families in which such contacts occur, and they can, obviously create all sorts of problems, emotional as well as legal. If any young person is in such a situation it's important he or she talks to someone reliable about it — a school counsellor, a social worker, a trusted family doctor. Seeking help may cause family ructions, but that will happen eventually anyway, and the needs of the young person involved are more important than the need to keep family peace.

It can be difficult, also, when young people become sexually involved with a step-parent. There may be no blood relationship, but it is still a prohibited sexual contact under the law. If the step-parent is one in name only — that is living with the young person's mother or father without being legally married such a contact isn't illegal, but it can still be explosive.

Sometimes young people whose original families have fractured become very confused about their feelings for their parents' new partners, and become involved with them in this potentially damaging way as part of their struggle to cope with their feelings. Once again, if it happens to you you would be best advised to talk in confidence to a person you can trust.

Sometimes young people become enamoured of an aunt or uncle, especially if they are close in age; it is distinctly possible to be a girl of sixteen with a glamorous young uncle of twenty or so. Again, *this is illegal*. Get help if you are involved in such a sexual relationship.

And, finally, there may be problems regarding in-laws. A girl who feels, deep down, some jealousy of an older sister may find that once that sister marries, she develops a crush on her brother-in-law, her sister's husband. It isn't so much that he's attractive — it's more a case of wanting to take from her sister something she values. If it happens to you, *be strong*. Back away hard, because you can gain nothing from such a relationship and can split your family in half. And if it's the other way round, and a brother (or sister) in-law makes a pass at you, again *back down*. If you think the situation through you'll know it's trouble looking for somewhere to happen.

Sex and violence

In the last few years, there has been a great deal of publicity about rape. It has become a major feminist issue, with some of the more militant women maintaining that rape happens not only when there is direct physical assault, but also whenever a man looks lasciviously at a woman. They say that women are always used by men as sexual objects and that women need to be aware of the sex war they are fighting. And so on.

I do not agree with this extreme point of view at all. I cannot see myself and therefore I can't see all women and girls as helpless vulnerable creatures swept aside by ungovernable male passion and cruelty.

Yes, of course some men are cruel and vicious. So are some women. But the majority of men can also be like the majority of women, tender and thoughtful and sensitive to their partners' needs from time to time (even the most caring will sometimes be selfish and thoughtless). It just doesn't help anyone to make blanket judgements about people on the basis of just one aspect of their personalities — and gender is only one very minor aspect.

So I am not going to solemnly warn girls reading this book that Boys Are Not To Be Trusted and that Rape is Inevitable unless you arm yourself with hatpins, pepper pots and a training in karate. But I am going to warn them that some boys and men, often those who have had a damaged childhood lacking in parental love and support, are unable to handle their sexual drives without being violent. And that for that reason:

It is not wise to wander alone in the middle of the night in dark and unpopulated streets and lanes.

It is not wise to climb into cars with men you don't know.

It is not wise to go off with a cheerful stranger who offers you the adult equivalent of sweeties.

It is not wise to strut about in really provocative, sexually-displaying clothes unless you want people to be sexually provoked, and can handle the results.

This advice has been offered to girls for years — indeed for centuries.
Our era is not uniquely violent, sexually or in any other way. Violence is a persistent strand of human behaviour and always has been, but we are in this twentieth century less violent and more compassionate than previous generations have been. But there are still some disturbed men who need avoidance — not because they are wicked men, but because they are sick men. You don't cuddle up to someone with smallpox, for fear of catching it, but that doesn't mean you have to hate the poor devil who has the disease.

If any girl feels she has been treated with violence by a sexual partner, she may need counselling, the talking-it-out treatment that helps many people handle painful experiences (see the back of the book for sources of help).

Promiscuous sex

One of the ideas that has been floating about during the last couple of decades is that it is ridiculous to assume that human beings are naturally monogamous — happy to spend the whole of their sex lives with just one sexual partner. Sex, the New Thinkers proclaimed, is just another appetite. Mankind can eat a wide range of foods, so mankind can enjoy a wide range of sexual partners.

Like so many New Ideas this one is very beguiling because it is half true. Indeed, yes, people can and do relate successfully to any number of different sexual partners. As I've already said, we aren't pieces of jigsaw puzzle looking for our matching halves.

But that doesn't mean we are going to be happy if we share sex with lots of different people.

Yes, some people can and do sleep around, going from partner to partner and after a quick bout saying cheerfully, "That was fun — see you around", and going on whistling happily to the next partner. By and large, the people who are able to do this are men — their biological drive to impregnate as many female animals as possible is programmed into them by a Nature anxious to keep the species going.

But not all men operate this way, and by no means all men who sometimes do, do so all their lives. We're the thinking animals, never forget. That means our thoughts and emotions alter our biological behaviour. And for a vast number of men really happy sex involves one life-long loved partner, and one only.

For girls this is often the case right from the start of their sex lives. Boys may go through a period of sleeping around before they fall in love — girls tend not to, again because of the biological drive to attach themselves to one safe male to give them babies. But remember that biological drive can be altered and in some girls it is. They do become promiscuous and sleep around with lots of different boys before finally falling in love and settling for one life-long partner.

Neither boys nor girls are wrong to do this. It's just the way they have chosen to behave, for whatever reason, and there is no point in others making judgements on them. There may be some problems however.

Some girls find they have difficulty in enjoying their own physical responses — they may fail to reach a climax because they don't have close enough relationships to allow it to happen. Some boys have a similar problem — they find they suffer from premature ejaculation — they can't make their sexual arousal last long enough to be satisfying to themselves or their partners.

Problems like this may need the help of a special kind of therapist (see the Information Section). Or people may be able to solve them themselves as they grow older and learn to understand their own responses better. Certainly they aren't problems that need make a person fear for his or her long-term health and happiness.

There is however another problem that does cause such fear and which is very much a risk of promiscuous sex — venereal diseases (as they used to be called) or sexually transmitted diseases, as they are now called. *These are dangerous.* They include syphilis and gonorrhoea, both of which can cause pain, generalised illness and most importantly, long-term sterility.

IT IS NOT POSSIBLE TO GET THESE DISEASES EXCEPT FROM A PERSON WHO IS ALREADY INFECTED: PEOPLE DO *NOT* USUALLY GET THEM FROM LAVATORY SEATS OR SOILED TOWELS OR POTS AND PANS OR MASTURBATION OR ANYTHING ELSE — *THEY GET THEM FROM ANOTHER PERSON.*

And a person who sleeps around is very likely to be a carrier. A couple who are both virgins, both love each other, and decide to make love and never make love with anyone else are totally free from risk. It is not sex itself which causes STDs — it is sex with infected people.

If you have had sexual contact with a person you suspect may have had sex with others before you, then go to your nearest Sexual Diseases Clinic where you can get totally confidential advice, whatever age you are (see Information Section). Parents and teachers are never told you have sought treatment.

Other people's sex

Girls and boys aren't involved only with their own and each other's sexual feelings. They are also very much involved with those of their parents and other adult relatives. And it's important they remember that.

Because too often young people, newly entered into their own adult sexuality, think they have invented sex when of course all they've done is discovered it. They assume that anyone over the age of thirty or so is really too old for sex, that there is something rather ridiculous about people of forty or more having sexual appetites, and something downright disgusting about sex and the over sixties. (Incidentally, there is no "normal" strike rate for having sex: the level of desire or need varies from person to person.)

This is all poppycock. Sex is important at all stages of human life — remember, we use sex as a game, and not just for reproduction — and your sort of young sex is not all that different from older sex. Your parents have as much right to sexuality as you have, and so have your grandparents.

Having said that adult sex and young sex are part of the same package, I must now go on and point out that in time adult sexual experience changes. The high drive and responsiveness of youth tends to ease off — not because older people are "past it" but because they become used to it, even bored. You may think at sixteen that it is impossible for sex ever to get boring. I know I did. But you will discover, as I did, that there are indeed times when you'd just as soon have a nice cup of tea and a long snooze as a passionate tumble in a silken bed.

Some of this loss of interest in women may be based not on boredom, but on hormone changes. Just as the onset of puberty in girls brings with its new hormone levels new sexual awareness, so do the hormone changes of the menopause bring about alterations in sexual response. Some older women may become edgy and unhappy about sexuality and feel less than energetic and well — and they, if they are faced with a busy, sexy, full-of-energy daughter or granddaughter can become very hard to get on with indeed.

Men, though they don't have a menopause (men don't have periods and the word menopause means "end of periods") may have a mid-life crisis, a time when they look at their lives and achievements and perhaps find them less than satisfying. They may find sex is dull, that the future is less attractive than the past, and the result can be, in a man who has sons or grandsons, a very explosive situation indeed. The household resounds to the roar of clashing personalities.

Also, men who are fathers may sometimes find their biology makes them respond with sexy feeling to people their education and intellect tell them they should not respond to — like their own daughters. Men to whom this happens sometimes get very agitated indeed, and imagine there is something very dreadfully wrong with them. They may be so horrified by these unexpected reactions that they bury them deep in their subconscious minds and refuse to admit they are there. But they will emerge, of course — as anger directed at the person who caused the "bad" feelings in the first place — the daughter.

Which is why a girl can be bewildered by the changes in the dad who used to be so loving and affectionate. He calls her "scrubber" and "tart" or worse, accuses her of being a sexual slut, suspects all her boyfriends, tries to keep her shut up at home instead of allowing her to go out with her friends, and generally makes her life — and his own and everyone else's come to that — a misery.

It's hell to deal with, if you're the girl in the case. All you can do is be patient, to try not to be hurt — hard though that is — and to see it for what it is. Love turned sideways.

In time, with goodwill, most such fathers can be helped to see they are being unjust and will relax. Especially if they have a sensible wife to help them do it.

But women too get such problems. There are mothers who treat a newly developed daughter harshly, accusing her of sexual misdemeanours, not because the girl is truly "immoral", but because of an unadmitted jealousy of her youth. It's natural and absolutely normal to be envious of the child who still has all the young sexiness that you yourself have mislaid. But it is sad if it makes you unkind to your own child — but it happens.

Again, if the girl can be patient, and refuses to allow her self-esteem to be too damaged, such mothers usually learn to change their behaviour.

But if the problems go on, then once again, it's counselling you need — that supportive outside help from someone who does understand how you feel and who does care. (See Information Section.)

QUESTIONS

Question 1   "I am 16 and in my last year at school, and a year after I've left I'm going to get married. The trouble is I'm a virgin and my future husband thinks I am not, because one night I was at his house and he started kissing my neck. He went on down and I flinched back because he wanted to go all the way and I said quickly and nervously, 'No'. He sat up and said, 'You're not a virgin, are you?' I replied, 'No! I just don't want to take any risks.' I had to lie because I thought he might lose interest. So now I've lied I'll have to carry on. Please don't try to make me talk to him about it, because I'm scared of what his reaction will be. I don't know how I can prevent him from finding out that I am a virgin. I read somewhere that vibrators can be used to break a girl's virginity. Where could I get hold of one?"

Answer It's not a vibrator you need but a good deal more common sense! Why on earth should you be ashamed of the fact that you are a virgin? It's nothing to hide, any more than loss of it is anything to boast about. Of course I'm going to tell you to talk to your fiancé. You can't possibly contemplate marrying a man you can't talk to on so important a subject. He may be a little hurt that you lied to him, but it's such a silly lie that it's my guess he'll understand and forgive it. And something else you should talk to him about is the fact that you're so very young to be getting married. You need time to grow up properly, to get to know yourself and to develop some mature self-confidence before you settle down to domesticity. You should be thinking now about what sort of work you'll do when you leave school, rather than planning a wedding.

Question 2 "I am a sixteen-year-old girl. I am very quiet and shy. I have to know people really, really well before I can talk with them. I can only be casual and talkative with people after I've had a couple of Baccardi and Cokes (which is the only alcoholic drink I like!). I could almost cry sometimes I get so embarrassed when I have to dance at parties, etc. Although I hardly have anything to do with boys, I often imagine I have sex with different teachers, actors, etc. Please help me. Surely I shouldn't think about sex as much as I do. Also, please don't laugh but I'm forever pretending I'm famous. Whenever I feel depressed I always make believe it's the pressure of being famous. I know I'm pathetic, but I *practically live my life with this fantasy. I'm terribly worried I'm a freak that'll end up on the shelf."*

Answer You're worrying about quite the wrong things. Your shyness is absolutely normal. At 16 more people are quiet and shy than are life-and-soul-of-the-party types. Your preoccupation with sex is totally normal too, because your body is fully grown, even though your social skills and emotions aren't yet, and is clamouring for adult living. But because you aren't ready yet for real sex, you're doing what we all did at your age — dreaming about it. And very nice too. Those daydreams can be smashing. As for the fantasy about fame — that too is a normal expression of your hunger to be up and about on your own life, and shows that somewhere inside you there's a lot of ambition that could take you on to a great future. But — and this is the worrying bit — *using alcohol to cushion the pains of growing up is going to ruin that future.* You do not need booze to make you lively and interesting. There's nothing you get from a bottle that isn't really inside you all the time. If you relax and give yourself time you'll develop your ability to chatter and be interesting without such a destructive crutch. I here make you a promise. You are not a freak and you can have a happy future, as long as you stop drinking right *now*.

Question 3 *"I love my girlfriend very much, and we both feel we're ready for sex. There's just one thing holding me back. I'm six-foot-two-inches tall and she's only five-foot-three and small with it. I'm quite well endowed sexually and when I'm ready for sex, frankly I think I'm very big. And I'm so worried I'll hurt her, because she's so little. She's a bit nervous too, I think."*

Answer Overall body size has hardly any relation to the size of the penis. Small men may have large ones, large men small ones. And whatever size the relaxed penis may be, when erect they're all much the same. So you are very unlikely to be unusually big. *And even if you were it wouldn't matter.* A woman's vagina is a most remarkable structure, of great elasticity. It is designed to allow the passage of a baby — and no man, however "well endowed", can match the size of a full-term baby's head. There can never, therefore, be any disproportion between penis and vagina size. There can however be tension and anxiety in a girl that makes her vaginal muscles go into a tight spasm which refuses entry to the penis, and causes severe pain if a man persists in pushing — but that is not a physical problem so much as a psychological one. If you and your girlfriend are both really sure you want to share sex, feel safe, emotionally and of course contraceptively, if you take your time and enjoy lots of preliminary love-play so that you are both fully aroused and ready for sex, then you should have no difficulties.

Question 4 *"I've never had sex with a girl, though I'm 17, and one of my mates told a girl he knew and she was sorry for me and said she didn't mind, so it was arranged we'd get together. But when it came to it I just couldn't. I don't mean I didn't want to — I did. It was just that I couldn't get an erection, though I've never had any trouble like that when I've masturbated. I often wake in the morning with one. But with a real girl I just got nowhere. I feel really rotten. Does this mean I'm impotent?"*

Answer No, of course it doesn't! It just means that you're a normal chap who needs a real relationship with a girl he knows and likes before he can relax enough to allow his body to behave as it wants to. To be thrust into a confrontation with a total stranger and expected to perform like a bull in a field is no way to help a young man feel sexually confident. There is nothing to fear about your potency, I assure you — and there is also nothing to fear about being a virgin of 17. It's no shame to be sexually inexperienced. You don't have to be pitied just because you haven't yet found the person with whom you want to share this experience. So I'd ignore your rather silly mate and his so-called help, and look about you for a girl you can love. And then you'll have no problems.

Question 5 "I love my girlfriend very much and one day we're going to get married. And I've had lots of different girlfriends before her. But now I'm really scared stiff that I'm turning gay, because last night I dreamed I was having sex with a bloke. It really makes me sick to think about it. How can I go on with my girlfriend if I'm going to change like this?"

Answer Relax! You're not "turning gay" just because you had this dream. And may I say, incidentally, it's not a disaster to be homosexual. The world is full of happy successful people who happen to be gay and have no more problems than anyone else. But back to you and your dream — and I can tell you that everyone, whatever their sexual preferences during their waking hours, will dream at some time or other about sharing sex with their own gender. Both sexes enjoy the ability to respond warmly to anyone; both sexes are likely to experience times in their lives when they find a same-sex person physically arousing. *It's all normal.* People also dream about having sex with their own parents, sisters and brothers — all sorts! And that's all normal too. So forget your dream. It means nothing that need worry you.

Question 6 "I am a 15, nearly 16-year-old girl, and have been going out with my boyfriend now for seven months. I know it is illegal to have sex under 16, but the other day, my boyfriend asked me to make love with him. I love him a lot, but sometimes I wonder deep down in my heart if I really do love him. I know there must be many people my own age, and in the same situation as me."

Answer I'm sure you do love your boyfriend a lot. I'm sure he loves you a lot. But the fact that you feel loving doesn't mean you're ready for the full adult commitment of sex. And you clearly aren't, because it is this that is holding you back, not anxiety about the legal aspects. The simple answer to your dilemma lies in a very old North country proverb: "When in doubt, do *nowt*." In other words, listen to yourself, and follow your own feelings. They're telling you to take your time. And most sensible people of your own age will find that they'll get the same message from their inner feelings, if they'd only listen to them!

Question 7 "I am 18 and gay. I desperately need to talk to somebody who is in the same situation or someone who will understand. Nobody knows I am gay and I know it would deeply hurt my parents if they found out. I have nobody else to turn to, so could you please give me a telephone number, or an address I could go to where gay people meet?"

Answer You don't tell me whether you're a boy or a girl — and that is significant because this country's laws about homosexuality are so shamefully unjust. It is illegal for boys under 21 to be involved in homosexual practices, but not for girls. Crazy, isn't it? I can tell you, however, that whatever gender you are, there is a group that can advise you. Contact Gay Youth Movement, BM-GYM, London, WC1N 3XX, and also a very wise and caring lady called Rose Robertson, of Parents' Enquiry, 16 Honley Road, Catford, London SE6 2HZ, who will help your parents understand.

No doubt there are questions you have about sex that haven't been dealt with here. It's inevitable that there should be because it's a huge subject and there are a great number of questions. You'll find that if you go along to your local library there are many books that have been written on sex, and if you're interested you can set yourself a course of study.

All I want to add to what I have already said is a code of sex manners. Really, they're just basic good manners. If you apply the code to all your relationships, not just sexual ones, then the chances are you'll be behaving well towards others — and towards yourself.

Code of sex manners

THOU SHALT treat every person with whom you become involved with the same respect, tenderness and care you would like to be treated yourself.

THOU SHALT NOT assume that others feel as you do, or react as you do, or have the same needs you do. Everyone is an individual and deserves individual recognition.

THOU SHALT talk in depth with your sexual partners, sharing feelings and explanations and understanding. If you can't share your minds, then you can't share your bodies.

THOU SHALT NOT kiss and tell — whatever you and a sexual partner share is between you. To prattle to outsiders about someone else's sexual behaviour and reactions is as cruel as stripping them naked in public.

THOU SHALT be honest. Never pretend to loving feelings you don't have just to get your own sexual way. Never swear undying love unless you genuinely believe you feel it. Never promise to be the one and only if you don't mean it.

THOU SHALT NOT put on a show for a sexual partner, pretending to get a sexual response you don't, or pretending to feelings you don't experience. However hurtful it may be for a partner to be told the truth, it is never as painful as finding out you've been lied to.

THOU SHALT be generous in your sexual relationships, giving as much of your emotions, your care, your involvement as you genuinely can. When you concentrate on giving rather than on taking, with a partner who shares your efforts to follow this code, then both of you gain.

THOU SHALT NOT use sex as currency. To assume a girl must provide a boy with quick sexy thrills just because he's spent money taking her out or given her presents, is to practise a form of prostitution. To choose a sexual partner according to the size of car he drives, the money in his pocket or the splendour of her parents' home, is the pits. *Love should be given freely or not at all.*

THOU SHALT be as informed as you can about all aspects of sexuality, including contraception and the risks of disease, as well as the more exciting things like sexual techniques.

THOU SHALT NOT abuse another person's ignorance. To persuade someone to enter into some sort of sexual activity when he or she doesn't really know what they are letting themselves in for is the same as robbery.

CHAPTER NINE

YOU AND YOUR PLANS FOR THE FUTURE

QUESTIONS

Question 1 "I am a 17-year-old girl presently at college studying for my 'A' levels. I have attended college for five months but am unwilling to do the extra work required at this level. Would I be silly to leave if I can get a good job just because I cannot force myself to work and want to go out and enjoy myself?"

Answer If you can get a good job without adequate qualifications is the big question. In times of high unemployment the people who do best are the ones who have shown they are capable of hard work and application — and they tend to be the ones who have passed exams. To chuck up college because you don't feel like work could mean chucking up a happier future. You can study and still have fun, you know. Students don't have to spend all their time with their noses in books, if they plan their work sensibly. You'll find the college tutors can give you a lot of guidance on how to get the best of both worlds.

Question 2 "My $15\frac{1}{2}$-year-old daughter has met a boy of 19. She's been going out with him for about six weeks. She now tells me that when she is 16, she is going to leave home and live with him. Before she met this boy she was going to college for a nursery nurse course, to work with children. Now she has *abandoned that idea and is talking about getting a job in a shop. My husband says I am worrying about something that will never take place, but the hints my daughter keeps coming out with makes me think otherwise. Do you think I should wait and see what happens or approach the boy?"*

Answer But why assume that this boyfriend means an either or situation? It is possible for her to study for a career while living at home *and* to have a serious boyfriend. I know she's very young for so definite a commitment to one boy, but it does happen that some girls feel like this at an early age and if their parents try to resist them too hard, all they do is alienate them and drive them away from home. If you can help your daughter feel that you understand her need for her boyfriend and assure her that you won't try to separate them, she should be able to relax and go on with her plans to study, especially if you point out that becoming a trained nursery nurse is superb preparation for future marriage and motherhood. That could be attractive to her in her present starry-eyed state! So, yes, I do think you should talk to her boyfriend who, as a rather older and we hope slightly wiser person, should be able to back you up in encouraging her to go to college — and make it clear to her she can still live at home and have him as a boyfriend.

Question 3 *"I'm 14 and depressed. I have these ambitious notions of what to be when I grow up. I can't sleep without thinking about it, and then I begin to worry, in case it doesn't turn out as I plan. I'd like to have a glamorous job, and then I get afraid I'm going to end up behind a shop counter which I really don't want to happen. When I read books that I enjoy I end up feeling even more depressed, because I'd like to be the person in the story. I'd try talking to my mother but I don't think she would understand. I've tried talking to my friends at school, but I don't think they understand either. I read your column in the newspaper and I think you might understand."*

Answer Indeed I *do* understand. Your problem is one shared by a lot of intelligent, lively, ambitious people of your age, who look at their world and want the best for themselves from it. *And it's a great way to be.* The people who worry me are the couldn't-care-less types who never give a moment's thought to what they want to do with their lives. They're the ones who are all too likely to look back in later years and feel bitter with regrets at wasted opportunities. There is a lot you can do to cope with your feelings of depression. Set yourself goals that you can achieve and that could lead, in time, to the exciting and interesting job you want. Like working hard at school for CSEs and "O" levels, and later, for further qualifications. Above all, don't be ashamed or afraid of being ambitious. It's the fuel that will lift you off the launch pad into a good future.

They used to go on at me a lot, when I was young, about my future. About planning a career, and thinking about the sort of life I would have, and working hard to make it all happen. And sometimes I used to say, "Yes, my future — well, yes, all right — but what about my *now*?" and they'd tell me I was a silly child and didn't know what I was talking about and when I was their age I'd understand how important the future was.

Well, now I am their age, and I do know what I'm talking about, and I'm here to tell you I was right when I was younger. Your now is just as important as your future. The world is full of sad, ageing individuals who have spent so much time thinking about the life they will have to come, that they have had no joy out of the life they have already lived. And while it makes sense to save for a rainy day, it makes even more sense to be able to recognise when it's raining, and to start spending the savings.

But having said that, I have to admit that planning for the future is wise. Only a child can live the day just for itself, and give no thought to tomorrow. An adult can and should do both. So, how do you plan for tomorrow while making the most of today?

Further education

Going on to college or university or specialised training schemes can be the ideal answer to the unemployment problem for people who can handle the academic load. Of course there are some people who can't. It would be stupid to pretend that every young person is going to enjoy and benefit from such courses. But more can than they themselves may realise. Often young people label themselves as unable to take further education courses, and they do it for a number of reasons.

IF your own parents left school without ever considering going on to further education —

IF the majority of people in your neighbourhood and attending your school leave without ever considering the possibility of further education —

IF you've never had the chance to meet older students who have gone on to further education —

IF you've never really pushed your own abilities to their utmost —

You may take it for granted that further education is not for you.
And you may be taking for granted a load of old codswallop.
So give it a second thought — and if you think you stand a chance, have a go.

Choosing a career

Many of the choices people make at school and about further education are based on choices they have made about the career they want. This can make sense, of course; if you want to be a doctor, you'll need to do "A" level science, not art (not because doctors can't be artists too — but because the medical schools demand science "A" levels as their entry qualifications).

This is fine if you've known since you were three and a bit that you were born to be a doctor, or an accountant, or an engineer, or whatever. Then by all means stick to your choice, if you're certain that it's what you want (one word of warning: some people opt for careers because their parents have been telling them since they were three and a bit that this is the career that is best for them — so think hard; is this *your* choice, or someone else's?).

But what do you do about your choices in education if you aren't sure what career you want? If you really haven't worked out the career that would, you believe, give you most satisfaction? Then you can flounder badly, and end up either abandoning education altogether which is sadly wasteful, or opting for studies that are general and not particularly vocational (that is, aimed at a particular career).

All this means that you'll have to think about what you want. And think hard.

So how do you start thinking? Try this strategy.

STRATEGY
for choosing a career

1. Take a sheet of paper, and down one side make a list of all the things you *most dislike doing*. As an example my list would look something like this:

   Working alone
   Working in the open air
   Working with animals
   Working with figures
   Working solely with my hands.

   This list will show you what you'd hate to be. In my own case, it shows I'd be a disaster as a gamekeeper, a forester, a zoo official, a farmer, an accountant or a lathe operator. Your own list may be quite the opposite of course, but will work in the same way — it will exclude areas of activity that are useless to you.

2. Now make a list alongside the first one that shows the areas you feel you could be good at. Here is my example again.

   | Working alone | Working in a busy environment |
   | Working in the open air | Working in office/shop/factory |

Working with animals	Working with people
Working with figures	Working with words, written or spoken
Working solely with my hands	Working with my head more than with hands

This showed me that I could be happy as a writer, as a teacher, as a secretary, as a nurse, as a factory worker, as a shopkeeper's assistant, as a receptionist — and in fact, in my time I've been all of these things (before I trained as a nurse, I worked in shops and factories and offices, always in a lowly capacity; since nursing I have become a writer and broadcaster, particularly involved with teaching).

Your lists will show you the same areas of possibility. Your lists may well be much longer than mine — or shorter — but if you've put in all you can think of, you should have a springboard for further action.

3   Make a list of the careers you think you might enjoy, using the Career Information at the end of this book. Collect all the information you can about all the careers. Send a stamped addressed envelope to the organisations that interest you, asking them to send you all they can about necessary qualifications, training schemes, financial rewards, promotion prospects, etcetera.

4   Go to your local library and take out as many books as you can on the careers that interest you.

5 Make a chart like the one on the following pages, and fill in under each heading the information collected from your various sources.

6 Now set aside all the books and brochures and look only at your chart. You will see at a glance which careers are impossible for you. You will also see which are your most likely "best buys".

7 If there are still no obvious answers, it could be that you have not explored as many possible careers as you could have done — you limited your horizons too much. Back to the library and elsewhere and see if there are any others you could add to your chart.

8 *Have a go.* Set out to get the qualifications/ apply for entry to training/or whatever is the next relevant step.

9 *Keep your chart by you.* Then, if your first choice of career fizzles out — you can't manage to get the entry qualifications, or can't finance the training period — you can try again with another possibility.
Remember that many of the world's most successful and happy people have had tries at several different occupations before giving up work altogether, and retiring.

CAREER "BEST BUYS"

JOB TYPE	BASIC QUALIFICATIONS	TRAINING COST	TIME	INCOME
ACTOR				
ARCHITECT				
BEAUTICIAN				
CARPENTER				
DIETICIAN				
DOCTOR				
ENGINEER				
FASHION WRITER				
HAIRDRESSER				
JOURNALIST				
NURSE				
PHOTOGRAPHER				
PLUMBER				
SOLICITOR				
TAX INSPECTOR				
TRAVEL AGENT				
ETC.				
ETC.				

FUTURE PROSPECTS		TRAVEL OPPORTUNITIES	FREELANCE OPPORTUNITIES	ETC	ETC
ADVANCEMENT	SECURITY				

What about money?

There are people who consider the most important grounds on which to choose any activity is money. They are the people who can be content in any career as long as it pays enough. Well, of course, money is important. You can't get far in this world without it. But to choose a career on that basis alone is very short-sighted. There are other things, just as important as money, to consider — like what will interest you or give you satisfaction to do day after day. No amount of money is worth being bored for the rest of your working life, or having to work punishingly long hours.

If you can combine money with job satisfaction, that's marvellous. Otherwise, look before you leap.

Handling your money

Some people start earning their own money quite early in life. (I have a brother who, at the age of five, used to beg me to make him pretty paper aeroplanes. I did. And then discovered he was selling them at school for a penny each, a clear 100% profit. I knew then he would go far financially.) Some take Saturday jobs (see the Information Section for the law about employment for your age group). Some take on a paper round. Some persuade family and friends to pay them for household chores.

Whatever the source of your earnings, questions may now arise.

1 How much should you kick back at home?
2 How much should your parents continue to give you as pocket money?
3 How much control should parents exercise over your earnings?

Every household is likely to have its own views on the answers. In a millionaire's home (do you know any? I don't) it will be seen as perhaps reasonable for young earners to hold on to all they earn, plus whatever their wealthy father gives them, and that they should never have any controls set over them at all. If you can afford to be this sort of parent and can guarantee your offspring the same enormous income you have for the rest of their lives, fair enough. They need no financial training.

For the rest of us, however, it's rather different. Most of us need as young people to learn the financial facts of life.

Most of us as parents need to feel we have taught our children those facts.

Here is my own set of answers to those three questions.

ONE: If the household is in need of cash, then after due discussion between young earner and head-of-household, a set sum should be put aside from personal earnings to cover expenses the HoH used to cover. Like, clothes, entertainments, and holidays. I do not expect people in short time, casual employment, like a Saturday job, to kick back hard cash — though I might if I were badly off and needed the money to feed the family.

TWO: Once again this depends on family income. If it is a healthy one, I feel it is reasonable for parents to go on offering pocket money as well on the understanding that major personal expenditure now becomes the young earner's department — that he can't earn *and* get pocket money *and* have his boots/best clothes/holidays paid for by his parents.

THREE: I believe that, however poor, however rich the family, young people must be allowed to plan their expenditure for themselves. If parents are always hovering over their shoulders to point out bad buys and prevent their version of extravagance the young one will never learn.

People who are in employment, or in receipt of allowances (having left school) are in a different situation to pocket-money earners. They need to pay their share to the household for their keep. I believe this is the simplest method of sorting out how much:

The main breadwinner adds up the cost of mortgage or rent, very basic expenses such as light, heating, etc., and cost of food per person, and works out the resulting total as a percentage of weekly earnings. Then if the child looks at his/her money, adds up fares, lunches and *essential* work clothes (with no cheating here) and subtracts this from his/her earnings, then the contribution to the family exchequer should be the same percentage as the prime breadwinner's. If it works out that he has to spend 60-70% of his money to keep the family going, then that's the proportion of remaining earnings that the child should cough up. This means that if the family is well off and the prime breadwinner's basic costs add up to only 15% of the family income, then the child only pays 15% too. So everyone shares the burden fairly.

EXAMPLE

THE PRIME WAGE EARNER EARNS, SAY £100 per week NET		THE TEENAGER EARNS, SAY £65 per week NET	
Expenses		*Expenses*	
Rent/Mortgage	£20.00	Fares	£5.00
Heating ⎫		Clothes	£7.50
Rates ⎬	£12.50	Food (lunches)	£7.50
Lighting ⎭		Miscellaneous	£3.00
Food per person	£12.50		
	£45.00		£23.00

45% of income therefore is needed for basic living.

Therefore, teenager should contribute 45% of *remaining* income.
45% of £42.00 = approx £19.00
So, £19.00 should be his/her contribution to the kitty.

This is just an *example*; it is not meant to be used exactly. Basically the young earner offers the family budget the same *percentage* of his/her net pay after essential expenses as does the prime wage earner.

Savings

There are two sorts of saving; the first is *specific* — stashing away cash for a set purpose, be it a new record player, or Christmas presents for family and friends, or a ski-ing holiday next year.

And there is *general* — just stashing money away for a base fund, to be used in the future as and when need arises.

People wise in the ways of finance save both ways. They open bank deposit or building society accounts for general savings, and Post Office or bank current accounts for specific saving. Even if a person has only sixpence a week, he or she can do it — tuppence to spend, tuppence to save for a new bike, tuppence for a rainy day.

And do not think you have to be a certain age before you can open savings accounts. You do not. Banks will welcome you with open arms as a future customer as well as a present one however young you are. There are rules about withdrawals of cash for very young children —

which are there to ensure no unscrupulous person can use their money without their consent — but any bank manager will advise you on what is relevant for your age.

Choose a bank and go to a local branch and ask to see the manager — you may need to make an appointment. Explain you want to become a customer and explain your needs and note what the bank offers you.

Now, go to the local branch of the other major banks in your area and do the same. At the end choose which bank you want to join. It could be the one you like best is the one with the friendliest staff, or the one that offers what seems to be the best service (though there isn't a lot to choose between them in that in my opinion) or the one that is easiest for you to get to in banking hours. But take your time before you choose — and it's worth talking it over with your parents or someone else who knows about these things.

Insurance policies and the stock market and other such matters

It is possible to manipulate money you have earned in many different ways. There are young people who take out endowment policies, or who buy stocks and shares on the stock market (which is a form of gambling) or who want to become investors in other people's projects. All this is very complex. If your parents have an accountant, ask if you can talk to him about it. If not, try and find someone else who can give you good *independent* advice. Beware of those who are simply interested in selling their own schemes.

Unemployment

Discussion of money and possessions brings up the most painful fact of our times — which is that for a large number of young people gainful employment is exceedingly hard to find. Far too many young people are leaving schools and colleges ready to take jobs that will both fill their daily hours and give them an income, and finding that such jobs just aren't there.

But this is not new.

To assume there was a golden past when all young people got jobs easily and with them enough cash to be independent adults is nonsense. Until the "booming" Sixties and early Seventies, most youngsters worked hard for very little money. Very few indeed could expect to be able to pay rent for their own accommodation and feed and clothe themselves. They were as dependent on family money as any unemployed person today. Indeed, many of them worked appalling hours under very nasty conditions and ended up with less money in their pockets in real terms than unemployed young people getting the dole today.

So don't add to your distress at being unemployed by believing that you are part of a uniquely deprived generation. That lucky one to which your parents belonged was just that: *lucky*. There was full employment and money was easy. Talk to your grandparents if you want to know what it was really like to be young in the past.

But where you are deprived today if you're unemployed is in a sense of personal worth. For far too long we have valued people not for their personalities, their intelligence, or their warmth, but for what they do. Ask someone, "Tell me about Joe," and the answer is very unlikely to be, "He's a nice bloke — enjoys fishing and is fun to be with," but, "He's a plumber." Jobs have defined people for so long that many young people today define themselves in those terms. They feel because they haven't jobs that the reason is some lack in themselves, that they are unemployable, rather than that there just aren't enough jobs to go round. They diminish their own worth in their own eyes.

If you can rid yourself of this notion, you'll do your unemployed self a power of good. You'll also be able to find ways to use your time more gainfully than just sitting about hoping a job will turn up. You'll use your own interests, energies and tastes to fill your hours agreeably. You might be a gardener at heart, and be able to turn the family plot into a beautiful and productive thing. Growing vegetables can be pleasurable and profitable. Or you could learn to make your own clothes (try local evening classes or teach-yourself books) using materials from things you buy for very little at jumble sales or Oxfam-type shops. Or you could pick up bits of old furniture from junk shops and make them smart and servicable again. Remember that if you are unemployed in the classic sense then you are free to employ yourself and develop some of your own skills and talents.

How to leave home

Once people do start to earn — and of course many do, even though many can't — they come nearer to being ready to leave the parental home and setting up on their own. Some of course do so because they go to college or because they choose a career that demands "living-in", like nursing for example. Whatever the reason, how do you do it to make it easy for yourself — and for the family you'll be leaving behind?

Money: First things first — and careful budgeting is a must. Make sure you know how much you've got, what your essential outgoings are, and spend your money accordingly. Wise people always pay their essential bills as soon as they have their money. They also set aside each week in advance their vital expenses: food, heat and daily travel. Then, and only then, do they think about such matters as clothes and fun.

It also helps to have a vital contingency fund tucked away. You never know when you may need urgently the price of a ticket home. People get ill, remember, and family crises do arise.

Keeping a budget book may sound dull, but it's a sensible activity. Seeing how you spend your money helps you see if you're spending it well.

Food: The next most vital area, and one closely linked to the matter of money management, is planning how you'll eat. Living on a diet of coffee and breakfast cereal and take-away hamburgers is not only unhealthy — it's absurdly expensive. You get bad value for your money. If you've been well brought up you should be able to cook (of course, that's true for boys as well as girls!) and be able to put together a cheap and cheerful meal from inexpensive ingredients. A stew made of the cheapest cuts and lots of good root vegetables and seasoning is nutritious and real value for your money.

As for the how-to — in most student residences and young people's hostels there will be kitchen facilities, and in most bedsits there will be access to a kitchen. And there are lots of good cookery books available to tell you how to eat cheaply and well.

Shopping carefully is as important as cooking carefully. Most supermarkets will sell small one-person size portions of meat, fish, cheese and so on if you ask — the pre-packed goods on display, remember, are often packed on the premises. And for fruit and vegetables look for a local market. Try to shop in as much bulk as you can (allowing for storage in your room) because that is always cheaper. And plan ahead. That way you're less likely to be dispirited when you end the day and haven't anything organised, and less likely to blow your money on expensive eating out.

Keeping Clean: More forward planning here. When you no longer have access to the family washing-machine, it's all too easy to find suddenly that every stitch you possess is unfit to wear. The weekly visit to the launderette can ensure you're clean though you may still be crumpled if you haven't got an iron, or perhaps better still bought non-crease clothes.

And cleaning the room you live in is a must, too. If you're lucky enough to have a room in a residence where staff come and have a go, good for you. But you'll still need to deal with some yourself — so setting aside a regular weekly hour or so to tidy up will make sure you don't live in squalor. Remember that you may get used to your own mess — visitors may be repelled by it.

Friends: Which brings up the matter of a social life — an absolute must for young people living away from home. It's all too easy to slip into a slough of loneliness when you leave the friends of schooldays and childhood behind, especially if you move to a bedsit. Students are forced into contact with people of their own age, but the young worker in a bedsit, however, can become totally solitary, and has to make a conscious effort to get to know people.

If you're a cheerful gregarious type, a pub or disco may be all you need to launch you on the local social roundabout. If you're at all shy, they can be a hell. Better to go to the library or Citizens' Advice Bureau (address for this will be at your local Post Office) and get a list of local clubs for young people. And join some. It can be tough at first, but if you try, you can get to know one or two people and from then on you're on your way (see Chapter 6).

Homesickness: Whether you've left home to go to college or to work, whether you have hordes of new friends and activities or only a few, and whether you were happy living at home with Mum and Dad, or always fighting like Kilkenny cats, there will be times when you'll be hit by a very nasty illness indeed — homesickness.

It can vary from a mild attack of the weeps or glooms to a full blown misery. It can be brought on out of the blue by just hearing a familiar tune on the radio, or smelling a homely smell — like furniture polish, say — or just because it happens to be Sunday, and you think of everyone together at home without you.

Don't be frightened of it. You can ride the feeling, and start to enjoy lone life again, if you give yourself time and permission to miss your home. Phone them all and have a chat to reassure yourself they're still there and still love you. But do it too often and it not only costs a bomb — it increases the homesickness.

Then go to a film or a gig, call a friend, or go for a walk. Don't sit in your room and mope. That only makes the homesickness worse. Tell yourself you'll feel better tomorrow, and you will! The risk is that some people panic, think they'll always feel as miserable as this, and scuttle home. And then feel miserable there, because they feel they've spoiled the future — as in a sense they have.

* * *

So, you can cope with being an independent adult, can learn to have a new, happy relationship at home with Mum and Dad you now visit — if you get the basics right. That's why it's so important to work at the business of budgeting, learning to feed and clean yourself, and making new friends.

These are the props that will support you, as you create your new future. And when you've done that you'll be in a position to help Mum and Dad make their adjustments to your departure. Because however hard you may find it to leave home, be sure they're finding it even harder to lose you!

Epilogue

So, we've reached the end of my suggested route. I must repeat what I said at the start of this book: no one can do your growing up for you. It's your personal journey, and however many people have done it before you and will do it after you, it will be a totally unique experience for you. But the majority manage to get there, to grow up without falling to pieces or otherwise making a mess of it.

>So can you.
>Bon voyage.

INFORMATION SECTION

These addresses and other details are correct at the time of going to press, but they may change. Check at your local library or Citizens' Advice Bureau — and always enclose a S.A.E. when writing.

Counselling — Where to get it.

Social Services Department and *Citizens' Advice Bureau* — Local addresses in phone book or at Post Office.

Local Library often has notice board giving useful addresses. Also, Teachers, Youth Club Leaders, G.P., Local Religious Minister.

British Association for Counselling, 1a Little Church Street, Rugby, Warwicks. (List of local counselling and advisory centres 90p.)

National Association for Young Persons' Counselling and Advisory Services (NAYPCAS), 17—23 Albion Street, Leicester, LE1 6GD

Alcoholics Anonymous, 11 Redcliffe Gardens, London S.W.10 (local addresses in phone book)

Alateen (for children of alcoholics) and *Al-Anon Family Groups*, both at 61 Great Dover Street, London SE1 4YF.

British Pregnancy Advisory Service. Head Office: Austy Manor, Wooten Wawen, Solihull, West Midlands.

Brook Advisory Centres, 233 Tottenham Court Road, London W1P 9AE.

Campaign for Homosexual Equality (CHE), 274 Upper Street, London N1.

Family Planning Association — Information Service, 27—33 Mortimer Street, London W1N 7RJ.

International Social Service, 39 Brixton Road, London S.W.9. (can advise on marriage as a citizen of a foreign country)

Gay Youth Movement, BM/GYM, London WC1N 3XX.

Joint Council for the Welfare of Immigrants, 44 Theobalds Road, London W.C.1.

Marriage Guidance Council — local address in phone book.

National Council for One Parent Families, 255 Kentish Town Road, London N.W.5

National Society for Prevention of Cruelty to Children (NSPCC) 1 Riding House Street, London W.1.

Parents Enquiry (for parents of homosexual people) 16 Honley Road, Catford, London SE6 2HZ.

Samaritans — local number in the phone book. (Help the suicidal)

Standing Conference for Drug Abuse (SCODA) 3 Blackburn Road, London N.W.6. (Write for addresses of local groups)

Sexual Problems — See Brook Advisory Centres and Family Planning Association.

Sexual Transmitted Diseases — for local clinic addresses ring Town Hall Health Department.

Sexual Violence — Rape Crisis Centre
   London — P.O. Box 69, London WC1X 9NJ; 24 hr service 01 837 1600
   Birmingham — P.O. Box 558, Birmingham B3 2H1; Telephone 021 233 2122
   Manchester — P.O. Box 336, Manchester M60 2B5; Telephone 061 228 3602

      (Other areas, try local directory.)

Disabled

General

Disabled Living Foundation, 346 Kensington High Street, London W14 8NF.

Radar (Royal Association for Disability and Rehabilitation) 25 Mortimer Street, London W1N 8AB

190 *Growing Pains*

General advice: should always have up-to-date information on addresses of societies for specific disorders, e.g. epilepsy, multiple sclerosis, etc.

Blind

R.N.I.B. *(Royal National Institute for the Blind)*, 224 Great Portland Street, London W.1.

Deaf

R.N.I.D. *(Royal National Institute for the Deaf)*, 105 Gower Street, London W1E 6AH.

Sexual Problems

S.P.O.D. *(Sexual Problems of the Disabled)*, The Diorama, 14 Peto Place, London NW1 4DT.

Sport

British Sports Association for the Disabled, Stoke Mandeville Stadium, Harvey Road, Aylesbury, Bucks, HP21 8PP.

Students

National Bureau for Handicapped Students, 40 Brunswick Square, London WC1N

Slimming Clubs

Silhouette Slimming Club Ltd, 103 Harleston Road, Northampton NN5 7AQ

Slimming Magazine Slimming Clubs, 4 Clareville Grove, London SW7 5AR

Slenderquest Limited, Barnet Trading Estate, Park Road, Barnet, Herts.

Weight Watchers Ltd., 635—637 Ajax Avenue, Slough, Berks.

Education

Up till the age of 16

Information available from schools and/or Local Education Office (addresses in phone book).

Advisory Centre for Education (A.C.E.), 18 Victoria Park Square, London E.C.2.

After the age of 16

Information available from schools, Local Education Office, Careers Office, Job Centre (addresses in phone book).

Council for National Academic Awards, 3 Devonshire Street, London W.1. (publishes a list of courses, mostly at polytechnics).

Higher Education Information Centre, Middlesex Polytechnic, Queensway, Enfield (provides information on higher education courses and grants).

National Institute of Adult Education, 19b de Montfort Street, Leicester, LE1 7GE.

National Union of Students, 459 Holloway Road, London N7.

Open University, Walton Hall, Milton Keynes, MK7 6AA.

University Central Council on Admissions, P.O. Box 28, Cheltenham, Glos., GL20 1HX. (50p. for "How to Apply for Admission to a University").

Correspondence Courses

British Association of Correspondence Courses, 4/7 Chiswell Street, London E.C.1.

Council for the Accreditation of Correspondence Courses, 27 Marylebone Road, London N.W.1.

The National Extension College, 18 Brooklands Avenue, Cambridge.

Careers

Help is obtainable from Job Centres and Career Officers. There are various Government sponsored work experience and training schemes for the unemployed school leavers. Up-to-date information (provisions are changing all the time) available from Job Centres and Career Officers (addresses in local phone book).

Growing Pains

Books which may be helpful

TITLE	AUTHOR	PUBLISHER
Annual Careers Guide		H.M. Stationery Office, Atlantic House, Holborn Viaduct, London EC1P 1BN
Careers '84		NOP Publications, 76 St James's Lane, London N10 3RD
First Steps to a Career	Shepheard	Nat. Advisory Centre on Careers for Women, 251 Brompton Road, London SW3.
Equal Opportunities	Ruth Miller	Penguin Books Ltd., Bath Road, Harmondsworth, Middlesex UB7 ODA
Directory of Jobs & Careers Abroad		Vacation Work, 9 Park End Street, Oxford.
Careers Without O Levels	Margaret Korving, Jim Davidson	B.B.C. Publications, 35 Marylebone High Street, London W1M 4AA
The Other Careers (Arts & The Media)	Bygrave, Goodman, Fordham	Wildwood House Ltd., 115 Bayham Street, London NW1 OAL
Which Career?	Catherine Avert	Robert Hale Ltd., Clerkenwell House, 45–47 Clerkenwell Green, London, EC1R OHT
Your Choice at 16+, Your Choice at 17+, Careers Beyond a Degree		Careers Research Advisory Centre (CRAC) Bateman Street, Cambridge

Sports — National Organisations

Angling

National Federation of Anglers, 2 Wilson Street, Derby DE1 1PG.
National Anglers Council, 5 Cowgate, Peterborough, PE1 1LR.

Athletics

British Amateur Athletics Board, Francis House, Francis Street, London SW1P 1DE.
Women's Amateur Athletic Association, Francis House, Francis Street, London SW1P 1DE.

Boxing

Amateur Boxing Association, Francis House, Francis Street, London SW1P 1DE.

Chess

British Chess Federation, 9a Grand Parade, St Leonard's-on-Sea, East Sussex TN38 0DD.

Cricket

National Cricket Association, Lord's Ground, London NW8 8QN.

Cycling

British Cycling Federation, 16 Upper Woburn Place, London WC1H 0QE.
Cyclists' Touring Club, Cotterell House, 69 Meadrow, Godalming, Surrey.

Equestrianism

British Horse Society, British Equestrian Centre, Kenilworth, Warwickshire.

Football (Soccer)

Football Association, 16 Lancaster Gate, London W2 3LW

Football (Rugger)

British Amateur Rugby League Association, 3 Upperhead Row, Huddersfield, HD1 2JL
Rugby Football League, 180 Chapeltown Road, Leeds, LS7 4HT.
Rugby Football Union, Whitton Road, Twickenham, Middlesex, TW2 7RQ

Gymnastics

Amateur Gymnastics Association, 95 High Street (2nd Floor), Slough, SL1 1DH

Judo

British Judo Association, 70 Brompton Road, London S.W.3.

Karate

Martial Arts Commission, 4/16 Deptford Bridge, London SE8 4JB

Keep Fit

Keep Fit Association, 70 Brompton Road, London S.W.3.

Swimming

Amateur Swimming Association, Harold Fern House, Derby Square Loughborough, LE11 0AL
British Sub-Aqua Club, 4th Floor, 16 Woburn Place, London WC1.

Tennis (Lawn)

Lawn Tennis Association, Baron's Court, West Kensington, London W14 9EG.

Tennis (Table)

English Table Tennis Association, 21 Claremont, Hastings, East Sussex.

Youth Organisations

Combined Cadet Force Association, John Islip Street, London SW1P 4RR.
Army Cadet Force, Millbank, John Islip Street, London SW1P 4RR.

Association for Jewish Youth, 50 Lindley Street, London E1 3AX.
Boys' Brigade, Brigade House, Parsons Green, London SW6 4TH.
British Red Cross, 9 Grosvenor Crescent, London SW1X 7EJ.
British Trust for Conservation Volunteers (ages 16—65), 10—14 Duke Street, Reading, Berks.
Church Lads & Girls Brigade, 15 Etchingham Park Road, Finchley, London N3 2DU
Church Youth Fellowships, Falcon Court, Fleet Street, London EC4Y 1DB.
Girls' Brigade, Brigade House, Parsons Green, London SW6 4TH.
Girls' Friendly Society, 126 Queen's Gate, London SW7 5LJ.
Girls' Guides Association, 17—19 Buckingham Palace Road, London SW1W OPT.
Girls Venture Corps, Redhill Aerodrome, Kingsmill Lane, Redhill, Surrey RH1 5JY.
Methodist Association of Youth Clubs, 2 Chester House, Pages Lane, London N10 1PR.
National Association of Boys Clubs, 24 Highbury Grove, London N5 2EA.
National Association of Youth Clubs, 70 St Nicholas Circle, Leicester LE1 7NY.
National Federation of Eighteen Plus Groups, Nicholson House, Old Court Road, Newent, Gloucestershire.
National Federation of Young Farmers' Clubs, Y.F.C., Kenilworth, Warwicks, CV8 2LG
P.H.A.B. (Physically Handicapped and Able Bodied), 42 Devonshire Street, London W1N 2AP.
Rotoract (Junior Branch of Rotary Clubs) Sheen Lane House, Sheen Lane, London SW14 8AF (or contact local Rotary Club)
St. John Ambulance Brigade, 1 Grosvenor Crescent, London SW1X 7EF
Scottish Girls' Training Corps, 53 George Street, Edinburgh, EH2 2HT.
Scout Association, Baden-Powell House, Queen's Gate, London S.W.7.
Sea Cadet Corps, Broadway House, Broadway, London, SW19 1RL.
Task Force, 1 Thorpe Close, off Cambridge Gardens, London W10 5XL.
Welsh League of Youth (URDD GOBAITH CYMRU), Director J. Cyril Hughes, Swyddfa'r Urdd, Aberystwyth, Dyfed.
Y.H.A. (Youth Hostels Association) Trevelyan House, St. Albans, Herts, AL1 2DX

Y.M.C.A. (Young Men's Christian Association) 640 Forest Road, London E17 3DZ.
Young Conservatives, Conservative and Unionist Central Office, 32 Smith Square, London SW1P 3HH
Young Liberals, 1 Whitehall Place, London SW1A 2HE
Young Socialists, Transport House, Smith Square, London SW1P 3JA
Y.W.C.A. (Young Women's Christian Association) 2 Weymouth Street, London W1N 4AX

Organisations that will Help Regarding Your Rights

Citizens' Rights Office, 1 Macklin Street, London W.C.2. (Particularly with regard to Social Security.)
Commission for Racial Equality, 10–12 Allington Street, London S.W.1.
Equal Opportunities Commission, Overseas House, Quay Street, Manchester.
National Council for Civil Liberties, 21 Tabard Street, London SE1 4LA.
Northern Ireland Civil Rights Association, 2 Marquis Street, Belfast.
Scottish Council for Civil Liberties, 146 Holland Street, Glasgow, G2 4NG (In Scotland legal rights may be different.)

Legal Facts

You and Alcohol

A person may drink alcohol in private (i.e. in his parents' or a friend's home) from the age of five.

A person can enter a public house but not drink or buy alcohol there from the age of 14.

A person may enter a public house and drink with a meal beer, wine or perry, from the age of 16.

A person may buy drinks of any kind in a public house and consume them there and may also work in a bar from the age of 18.

You and the Armed Services

A person may join the armed services with parental consent at the age of 16, if a boy, at 17, if a girl.

A person of either sex may join the armed services without parental consent at the age of 18.

You and the Cinema

A person may see a film with a 'U' or 'A' certificate at the age of five.
A person may see a film with an 'AA' certificate at the age of 14.
A person may see a film with an 'X' certificate at the age of 18.
(There is no certification system nor legal rules about the ages at which children may see live theatre performances.)

You and Crime

A person may be convicted of a criminal offence at the age of 10; however, until the age of 14 the prosecution has to prove the person knew the difference between right and wrong when the crime was committed.

A person may be held to be fully responsible for a crime at the age of 14 and, if a boy, may be sent to a detention centre.

A person may be found guilty of rape, if a boy, from the age of 14.

A person may be sent to borstal, or to prison to await trial, if a boy, at the age of 15.

You and Drugs

A person of any age may not use, sell or possess drugs listed as Class A (Heroin, LSD, opium in any form, injectable amphetamines, "angel dust") Class B (Marijuana — pot — and all amphetamine type drugs — speed) or Class C (Mandrax and other stimulants).

A person may buy cigarettes for his/her personal use at the age of 16. (See above for rules regarding the drug alcohol.)

You and Education (Leaving School)

There are rules regarding leaving dates. These are:-
1 If a person's 16th birthday is between 1st September and 31st January, he/she cannot leave school until the end of the Spring term following his/her birthday.
2 If a person's 16th birthday is between 31st January and the Friday before the last Monday in May he/she cannot leave school until that Friday (the "May Leaving Date").
3 If a person's 16th birthday is between the May Leaving Date and the 1st September he/she can also leave on the May Leaving Date.

You and Employment

A person may not take paid employment under the age of 13.
A person may get a part-time job at the age of 13, but

may not work before 7 a.m. or after 7 p.m.;
may only work for two hours on a school day or Sunday;
may not work during school hours (9.0 a.m. — 4.30 p.m. or lunch time);
may work 5 hours on a Saturday or during school holidays, but not more than 25 hours a week.

A person aged 15 may work at a part-time job for up to eight hours a day or 35 hours a week.

A person aged 16 who has left school may usually work under the same conditions as an adult, but if still at school the Local Education Authority may impose conditions.

A person aged 17 may be a street trader.

A person after the age of 18 may work in a bar, betting shop or race track.

The Local Authority may have local bye-laws which may be stricter — a copy can be found at the Town Hall.

The Local Authority may refuse a young person permission to work if it considers the job will damage education or welfare.

Earnings are legally the property of the earner and not his/her parents.

You can be taxed but are unlikely to earn enough. Until a person is 18 the parent should make a return on his/her tax form unless the earner is taxed on the PAYE system. A parent has the right to claim the money from their child for any tax he/she has to pay.

You and Your Medical Care

A person may choose his/her own doctor and consent to medical treatment at the age of 16.

You and Sex

A person may consent to heterosexual sexual intercourse, if a girl, at the age of 16.

A person may marry with parental consent at the age of 16.

A person may seek the permission of a court to marry, if parents object, at the age of 16.

A person may enter a brothel, and live in it, at the age of 16.

A person may consent to homosexual activity, if a male, at the age of 21.

A person may marry without parental consent at the age of 18.